Praise for *Win*

"In *Win the World without Losing your Soul,* Dave Durand coaches his readers toward the ultimate home run — a fulfilling life worthy of a heavenly reward. Dave uses the right combination of relevant anecdotes and practical applications to show readers how to reach their potential and how to win the right way. Success, money, fame — all these things are unfulfilling without a purposeful life."

— **MIKE PIAZZA,** husband and father,
Major League Baseball player, retired

"Having worked with Dave for many years, I have always found his business and life perspectives to be very insightful. His book is proof positive of this — enjoy!"

— **MIKE LANCELLOT,** Retired President & CEO,
Vector Marketing/CUTCO Cutlery Corporations

"Durand redefines 'winning' by holding a mental mirror up to the reader. The reflection includes the reader, natural law, and spiritual certitude. He challenges, inspires, and guides in this worthwhile volume."

— **MARGARET FARROW,**
Former Lieutenant Governor of Wisconsin

"Dave's work in *Win the World* is right on. He lays out the framework for success without compromise."

—**ROB JETER,** Head Coach, University of
Wisconsin, Milwaukee, Men's Basketball

"This is a book of great depth and truth. It contains compelling and invaluable insights for anyone who wants to live a fulfilling life."

—**PATRICK LENCIONI,** President, The Table Group;
bestselling author, *The Five Dysfunctions of a Team*
and *Death by Meeting*

WIN THE WORLD

WITHOUT LOSING YOUR SOUL

DAVE DURAND

A Crossroad Book
The Crossroad Publishing Company
New York

The Crossroad Publishing Company
16 Penn Plaza – 481 Eighth Avenue, Suite 1550
New York, NY 10001

Printed in the United States of America on acid-free paper

The text of this book is set in 11/14.5 Sabon.

Library of Congress Cataloging-in-Publication Data
Durand, Dave.
    Win the world without losing your soul / Dave Durand.
       p. cm.
    ISBN 13: 978-0-8245-2601-6 (alk. paper)
    ISBN-10: 0-8245-2601-5 (alk. paper)
    1. Success – Religious aspects – Christianity. I. Title.
    BV4598.3.D875 2009
    170'.44 – dc22

                                          2008006385

1 2 3 4 5 6 7 8 9 10   14 13 12 11 10 09

CONTENTS

INTRODUCTION

A S A BUSINESS LEADER and career coach, I've had the privilege of working with more than a hundred thousand individuals from all walks of life: from Fortune 500 top executives to sales representatives, small business owners, secretaries, teachers, and parents. No matter who I'm working with, two questions always arise:

* How can I reach my full potential and achieve my dreams?
* Is it possible to gain and sustain success within the bounds of sound morality and ethics?

Nowadays these are hard questions. Newspapers are filled with scandalous stories about people, from entry-level employees to executives, manipulating systems and other people for personal gain, no matter the cost. Leaders at companies such as Enron and WorldCom have been willing to risk everything, including their employees' livelihood and retirement savings, to find ways to cheat the system for huge profits.

Of course, examples of people trading morality and ethics for personal gain and gratification are not limited to the boardroom. In sports, steroid scandals in baseball, cycling, and track and field have shown, if there was any doubt left in anyone's mind, how often people will cheat to gain an edge over their competition. In schools, students exhibit a rapidly growing trend of cheating and violence. In relationships, infidelity is increasingly common.

And yet, even when these people are caught and publicly exposed, the lure of instant, effortless success remains very powerful in our culture. Hundreds of relentless messages about the importance of living a glamorous and pleasure-filled life are pounded into our minds every day. These images and sounds influence the decisions and actions of large numbers of people.

But the truth is, people who pursue success at all costs not only don't succeed; they usually end up soulless — some go broke, but others end up lonely, depressed, unhappy, and oftentimes hated.

The good news is that it does not have to be that way.

Many good, hard-working people attain success in their relationships, professional life, and finances without stepping over the line. Not only do they not feel trapped by ethics; they claim to succeed precisely because of their moral code. They come to understand who they are and what they are meant to do in life, and they live to their fullest potential each and every day. These are the people who win the world without losing their souls.

Winning the world is not about becoming a king or queen. It's about maximizing the potential you have as an individual. This means developing your talents, leveraging your resources, and working within the natural law to attain success. Success means different things to different people. For some it means being an elementary school teacher or being a stay-at-home parent. For others it means becoming the most powerful and influential leader in a given industry. Surprisingly, an elementary school teacher and a high-powered executive have similar foundations and use compatible philosophies in order to reach their maximum potential. They both pursue the best version of themselves. *Win the World* invites you to become that best version of yourself and shows you how doing it the right way, through a commitment to excellence and morality, will lead to joy and happiness. It also explores why and how doing it the wrong way, by taking shortcuts and acting unethically, will lead to destruction and misery. By reading this book, you will be empowered to make changes in your life and to avoid common pitfalls that lead to self-destruction. Winning the world without losing your soul is predicated on courage and integrity. The early twentieth-century explorer Ernest Shackleton provides a great example of what it means to live out these principles. Just prior to World War I, Shackleton led an expedition to Antarctica to accomplish something that no one else ever had — to cross the South Pole. To recruit men for the expedition, Shackleton allegedly placed a very peculiar newspaper ad that read:

> *Dangerous work, inexhaustible hours, low pay, virtually no glory, cold, hunger, odds of success — low, but a great adventure . . . CALL!*

He received thousands of calls and led one of the most incredible expeditions in human history.

Contrast Shackleton's story with those of countless advertisers throughout the ages who have intentionally misled their customers with sweet, honeyed ads but vinegary products, services, and opportunities. From snake oil salesmen to the executives at Enron, they all failed because they misled the people who were most important. Shackleton's ad was honest and direct, like the man himself, and in the end, he and his crew were successful. His upfront approach ultimately saved lives. He established trust, which was desperately needed countless times on that journey. (At one point, his mission met disaster after his ship froze solid on the ocean surface in the dangerous Antarctic! It was the crew's trust in their leaders and in each other that helped them survive.)

In *Win the World*, we explore the moral and ethical code exhibited by people such as Shackleton, and how you can apply it to your own life to achieve true success. We'll examine the difference between the mind-set and actions of people who live with long-range purpose and their counterparts who fixate on immediate gratification.

In answer to the questions above: yes, you *can* accomplish the greatest success in politics, education, parenting, in acting, sports, business, or wherever your passion is, *and* maintain your integrity.

Think of it this way. A boxer who wins a fight by bribing the referee may not be a good fighter. He is not necessarily tough, skilled, fit, or determined. And no matter how good he is, cheating would make people question his abilities. But a boxer who wins based on strategy, skill, and physical ability is respected for his accomplishments in the ring. And his success is not just a one-shot deal. By training to win the right way, he also develops the tools to fight, and win, again and again.

Winning the world the right way is similar. As we'll see again and again, *the end does not justify the means* — ever. Keeping this fact in mind will actually accelerate your journey to success by keeping you focused on who you are and what is relevant to living out your true vocation.

Each of us has a specific purpose and finite amount of potential. This book is not about the eternal consequences associated with selling your soul to achieve success, although like many people I believe those consequences exist. Rather, it's about learning how to explore your gifts and identify your purpose, so that you can fulfill your dreams with honesty and integrity during your earthly life. Any other way only leads to a lack of productivity and even destructiveness.

It never ceases to amaze me how liberating it is for people to realize that they have more potential and a greater purpose than they give themselves credit for. As this book guides you to discover for yourself, identifying your true purpose and tapping into your true potential is more powerful than any shortcut or scam ever will be. So, take this opportunity to pause and assess who you are and who you want to be, where you are going and where you want to be going, and how you can be your best self in an ethical and caring manner each and every day. By living with integrity, you can (and will!) win the world without losing your soul.

❧ *Chapter One* ❧

YOU ARE OBLIGATED
TO WIN THE WORLD

T HE GOOD NEWS is that, believe it or not, you *can* win the world without losing your soul. This may not come as a complete surprise. After all, if you didn't think it was possible, you probably wouldn't be reading this book in the first place. But what may surprise you is that, like it or not, you are *obligated* to win the world without losing your soul. You can run from your obligation, but unhappiness and despair will eventually find you. So winning the world is not about becoming a superhuman, someone more than you were meant to be. It's about becoming exactly who you are meant to be.

Winning the world is about reaching your maximum potential. But as you've probably learned in life already, making a commitment to being the best you can be may come with risks. Losing your soul happens when you abandon your purpose or pursue it with compromised principles. It happens when you decide to let the end justify the means. Although winning the world may sound like a daunting task, you were born with the potential to accomplish that mission. In your own unique way, you can pursue the task and, in the end, receive a reward that is beyond imagination.

Technology is a beautiful thing — until it doesn't work. Many of us know the feeling of frustration that accompanies a computer crash. In an instant, a tool designed to increase efficiency becomes an apparatus of *de*ficiency. And in many cases, when a computer fails, the consequences aren't neutral; they're negative.

The same holds true for people. When you fail to do what you were designed to do, the consequences are not neutral; they are negative. When you fail to love, people get hurt. When you fail to do your job, at a minimum, your company and coworkers suffer; at worst, you get fired. When you fail to take care of your body, you get sick. When you fail to use your natural talents and gifts, you begin a process of mental and emotional turmoil. Given enough time, this will lead to a lack of satisfaction in life, depression, and eventually death.

Most people fail to realize the magnitude of their responsibility to maximize their potential and use their gifts. You have a very specialized and unique design, which is meant to serve a purpose. You have an obligation to explore your purpose and then to live it out.

Each of us has a different set of natural talents, temperaments, personalities, and interests. This is not hard to recognize in the workplace and in social settings, but it is even more pronounced within families.

Recently, in order to get some father-and-son time, I took my two oldest boys with me to a series of speeches I was giving at the Baltimore Convention Center. They sat in on one of the talks. From the podium, I made the same point I am making right now about innate differences. I told the audience that my fourteen-year-old, who is very athletic, was probably in the back of the room thinking about how great it would be to clear out the chairs in order to start a pick-up game. I contrasted that with my ten-year-old, who thinks with a unique blend of creative engineering, by saying that he was probably thinking, "I bet this place is big enough to build an indoor roller coaster." The audience found the comment amusing, and so did my boys. Later that evening, my little engineer looked at me and said, "Dad, you were wrong. I wasn't thinking about a roller coaster. I was thinking about how to design a man-sized wind-up car."

Where do these interests come from? Why do we all have innately different attitudes about specific things like work, sports, and art? No doubt, as we go through life our experiences do shape our attitudes, but overall each of us has an inherent set of unique interests.

None of us has ever customized our own DNA. Our height, natural weight, looks, undeveloped natural talents, and temperament were all outside of our control. Nothing that is made is made without a purpose. And everything that is made is designed to meet the specific needs of the purpose for which it was made.

So part of winning the world is beginning with some basic self-reflection about who we are. Self-discovery reveals that, by design, we all have natural strengths and weaknesses. Personally, I recognize that there are some things I'm not naturally inclined to do. For example, I would be the world's worst doctor. My gross-out capacity would render me useless. I'd gasp and say, "Oooh . . . that looks really bad. Cover it up. It's making me sick." Nobody needs a doctor like that. But I'm grateful there are men and women who are naturally equipped to handle tough medical situations.

Today it's becoming more difficult for people to explore their strengths and weaknesses in an overall sense because Americans live in an age of virtually unlimited opportunity. It is difficult to discover your purpose in the midst of irrelevant distractions and choices. Choices are good, but the static that accompanies them can be a problem. Never before in history have people had more careers to choose from than they do today. A century and a half ago, which is a blink in time historically speaking, a young man could aspire to becoming a farmer, a tradesman, or . . . a farmer. This is an exaggeration, but it's no exaggeration to say that the choices were much more limited. Today, there are hundreds of careers one can choose from, many of which didn't exist at the beginning of the twentieth century, including fast-food management, software programming, media content production, systems analysis, and even new forms of mathematics — not to mention aromatherapy. And even the traditional jobs such as farming are vastly more complicated and technologically demanding than they were even thirty years ago, let alone a hundred years ago.

The fact that there are more choices is a good thing, but the confusion that accompanies these choices is not good. The dissatisfaction that people feel in their current careers is demonstrated by the way that people change jobs far more than they did fifty years ago, when it was more common to find a job and stay with it throughout one's life. While many of these changes result from changes in industry, increased job and career changes are also a sign that many people today exchange their purpose for a job. Such people look for the short-term gratification of a pay-check or even recognition vs. the long-term satisfaction of a purposeful career or vocation.

This should come as no surprise, considering that the same society has gone from having no TV channels at all to over a thousand channels and still claims to be bored. We complain that fast food is not fast enough and that owning a home, two TVs, and two cars is "barely get-ting by." After observing the growing dissatisfaction and higher standards of consumers, I'm convinced that human nature has a short attention span for gratefulness. I'm also convinced that it would take only a few months for a caveman zapped into the modern day to go from being grateful for the luxuries of today, such as running water and refrigeration, to complaining about slow service at a drive-through window.

In addition to each of our custom designs, we all have a natural desire to use those gifts. We all have a drive to *do something.* Some people use their drive to invent, like Thomas Edison or Benjamin Franklin. Others use their drive to conquer, like Attila the Hun or Hitler. Still others use their drive to climb Mount Everest or cross the Sa-hara. Some people put all their energy into pleasing people around them, while others put all their energy into master-ing a video game or surfing the Internet for pornography. Both evil and good are achieved from personal drive.

Like everyone, you have some achievements under your belt. What has the outcome of these achievements been?

What are you trying to "win"? Are you a better person with each victory? Will the world be a better place when you reach your objective? Have you found peace with your accomplishments, or do you feel empty even after your victories?

Examples of how reaching goals may not always bring good are plentiful. How could Hollywood be so filled with money, power, and fame yet be so famished for satisfaction? A young woman who dreams of being on the big screen never dreams about being married five times. She does not set out to become addicted to heroin and to commit suicide.

Initially, she wants to win the world of entertainment, but she doesn't want to lose her soul in the process. Even after she succumbs to the temptations of the world, deep down she wants to be freed from them. When she uses her talent for acting in a dignified way, she is happy. When she is exploited, she is miserable. In other words, when her talent is used for its intended purpose, the result is good. On the other hand, when her talent is used for a purpose for which it was not intended, pain follows.

In acting, and also in leading, teaching, parenting, or any other vocation, there will be temptations. The desire to cut corners will always be there. And so you might be tempted to go to the other extreme, denying your own natural gifts in order to play it safe. The fear of getting caught up in the Hollywood scene, for example, and succumbing to drugs or selling out to vanity has prevented potential Oscar winners from ever auditioning. But if you fail to pursue your purpose and to develop your gifts, you lose the world *and* lose your soul, because emptiness will set in. If your gift is acting, then act. Just find a way to do it in accordance with your purpose by equipping yourself with the means to defend against vice.

It's important to remind yourself that you are a one-of-a-kind, custom-designed individual and that no one other than you can put your natural gifts and talents into action. That is solely your responsibility. What would have happened if Joan of Arc had decided not to follow her heart and failed to liberate the French? An entire country's future would have been altered or possibly even eliminated. She could have reasoned that she was only a seventeen-year-old girl who had no business leading an army. She could have run away out of fear of being shot through the heart or maimed for life in battle. She had her entire life ahead of her, but she followed her conscience and rose up to be a great leader.

What would have happened if one of the great pioneers in treating cancer had started his research five years later because he just wanted to kick back and enjoy life for a while? How many people do you know who are living today because of cancer procedures that are only a few years old? And how many of them would not have survived if great pioneers hadn't started when they did? Or what if every great discovery in personal computing and Internet development had been postponed twenty years? We'd all be sitting around today using primitive forms of word processing, accounting software, and schedule management, and only a tiny few in the world would know how a new technology of "e-mail" might one day make it inexpensive to communicate around the world.

Most of us will not single-handedly lead an army on to victory after victory for the cause of justice or liberation, find a cure for disease, or create massive changes to technology, but we all play a role in the way the world works. Recognizing Christopher Columbus for his discovery of the new world for Europe is justified, but we should also recognize people like King Ferdinand and Queen Isabella of Spain for backing the exploration in the first place. Without their blessing, things would be quite different in the world today. No doubt America would have been discovered, but by whom? What if America had been discovered by explorers from the Far East or the Middle East? What would the world map look like today if the United States of America had never existed? Who would be in power?

Many people played a role in Columbus's discovery, including his parents, educators, shipbuilders, and crew. They may not be in history books, but they did make history. Each of us has a role to play in shaping the future for someone in some way. Winning the world is about maximizing your potential and taking action. It is about exploring your capacity, applying your talents, and developing your skills. As a human being, you have finite talent, but it is perfectly suited to the number of days that you have to develop it. Every day that you fail to live up to your potential will add to a surplus of potential at the end of your life. Your excess potential can't be used after you die — so use it now!

∞ Chapter Two ∞

MAXIMIZE YOUR CURRENT CAPACITY AND YOUR LONG-TERM POTENTIAL

I N THE LONG TERM, winning the world is about reaching your maximum potential. In the short term, it's about using your current capacity. The current capacity you have for work, physical activity, love, hate, greed, charity, sacrifice, knowledge, success, and many other categories is well beyond what you might imagine. The challenge is to focus on your capacity for good and productive endeavors. The good news is that you can use all of your current capacity today, whereas actualizing your maximum potential may take years and even decades to achieve.

Winning the world is about understanding the difference between your current capacity and your overall potential, and maximizing both.

It doesn't matter who you are, what you do, or what kind of family you were born into, you are capable of far more than you think. Even when people are good at focusing on their lifelong potential, they sometimes underestimate their immediate capacity. Some of us find ourselves in circumstances we never intended to be in. This can lead us to feel smaller than we are, or it can force us to tap more deeply into capacities we didn't even know we had.

There are countless examples of people who discovered that they were capable of more than they dreamed. There are people like Jackie Pflug. Teaching at the Cairo American School in 1985, she boarded Egypt Air Flight 648, ready to enjoy a weekend getaway. Her plane was taken over by Islamic terrorists, and she was shot in the back of the head, execution-style. Miraculously, she survived what ended up being one of the most horrifying and deadly hijackings in aviation history.

Jackie endured the emotional trauma of witnessing the terrorists search her fellow passengers for their paperwork. They were targeting Jews first, then Americans. Anyone found guilty of "the crime" of being a Jew or an American was forced to wait in line near the door of the airplane. After a few minutes, a new person was called up, each one shot in the back of the head with a .38, and thrown out of the plane.

The miracle of Jackie's surviving the impact of the bullet is amazing in itself, but her heroism, the depth of her real-time capacity, began after that event. Although she lay bleeding on the tarmac next to dead bodies, she remained calm. Hours later when the emergency crew arrived at the scene, she faked being dead, out of fear that the workers were really terrorists. While they were transporting Jackie to the morgue, Emergency Medical Technicians noticed that she was still breathing and immediately rerouted their vehicle to the hospital.

Jackie's recovery has been difficult, affecting, among other things, her short-term memory and her vision. But instead of harboring bitterness, she flies around the country, telling her story to inspire others to persevere during challenging times.

When you read Jackie's story, you might think to yourself, "I would never survive an experience like that." But can you really say that for sure? Jackie may have felt the same way about herself prior to her experience. Yet, when faced with a horrific situation, she had a greater capacity to deal with trauma, pain, and sheer terror than she ever would have expected of herself. And she did not work up to it, either. She didn't imagine it in the distant future and develop this threshold over a period of time. It simply existed inside of her, and only a major event proved how deep her capacities were.

Although most of us will never need to put our capacity to such an abrupt test, it does dwell within us and can be put to use immediately. For nearly two decades, I've helped people explore their capacity. It's gratifying work because, unlike the protracted time that it takes to develop potential, I get to help people start using their capacity immediately.

Think about the relationship between long-term potential and current capacity this way. Your potential is how far and fast you could eventually run with the right training and diet. Your capacity is how far you can run today. You may argue that you're so out of shape, you could only run two hundred yards before having a heart attack. Physically speaking, you may be right, but most of the time, when it comes to physical exertions, the will ends before the capacity of the body is reached. That is why coaches push athletes further than they want to go or believe they can go.

The limited conscious effort you put into running may make you believe that your physical capacity is limited. But consider the fact that your unconscious mind is already engaged in using your physical body to accomplish things well beyond your expectations. If you were to consciously manage your entire physical life according to the same self-imposed low standards that tell you how far you can run, you would sell your body short. Imagine. Your heart beats about a hundred thousand times per day.* When you're infected with a disease, your body sends antibodies to your defense. They attach to bad cells and discard them. You have as many as three hundred thousand platelets in your body working as an army to prevent you from bleeding to death when you are injured. These are all easy-to-accept facts because knowledge of them doesn't mean you need to do any more work. They happen on their own. Even if you don't believe these facts to be true, they will keep happening, and they're still true.

Just as you're designed to handle physical challenges well beyond your expectations, the same holds true on an intellectual and emotional level. The problem is that most of us walk around like we are underperforming PDAs (personal digital assistants). The average PDA today holds incredible quantities of information and has hundreds of functions, yet most PDA users, myself included, use them for little more than making and receiving phone calls and

---

*Steven L. Jacobs, *Whelmers: Science Demonstrations That Spark Your Imagination* (Wichita, KS: Oakland Avenue Science Supply, 1994).

for storing numbers. The PDA has capacity and potential. Its capacity out of the box is already more sophisticated than most users. Its potential is massive because it can be upgraded with different software packages. The creators of each new PDA probably agonize as they watch people like me waste the capacity and potential of their products. If my PDA had consciousness, it would be insulted and unfulfilled by my lack of complex commands. It would feel like Einstein working in a toll booth!

Your brain is capable of having more ideas than the number of atoms in the known universe.* It is difficult to avoid considering the idea that you might have an obligation to fill up some of that capacity. Reflect on the fact that the number of internal thought pathways your brain is capable of producing is one followed by almost 7 million miles of standard typewritten zeroes. Can this inspire you to get your mental construction equipment out of storage? The simple fact is that *at this very moment* you are capable of far more than you could imagine. Unlike learning about your physical capacity to heal, the revelation about your mental capacities may spur your conscience. Certainly, you don't need to train your body to heal itself, but you do need to train your mind to learn. Of course, much of that learning takes place unconsciously, but meaningful gains have a tendency to be made consciously. In other words, it will take effort, and that is why you may find yourself wanting to deny your capacity.

Would you ever go out and spend over $1 billion on a computer that can process more information than any

---

*Tony Buzan, *Head Strong: How to Get Physically and Mentally Fit* (New York: HarperCollins, 2001).

known piece of technology owned by any company, military, or government, and then simply use it to play *Pong*? Of course not. But if it were possible to build a computer with the capacity that your brain has, it would cost far more than $1 billion to produce. At this point, technology is not even close to developing it.

You walk around with a tool for learning that is invaluable. Use it that way. Most people never stop to consider the depths of their potential. They settle for an average life and wait it out until they die. If you don't want this to be your fate, take this opportunity to contemplate your present capacity and your long-term potential. Then make it a discipline to do so regularly. Ask yourself, what is the depth of understanding you could have about science, medicine, engineering, parenting, teaching, politics, philosophy, gardening, plumbing, or theology? How far could you run? How fast could you read? How deeply could you love?

Having a large family invites unsolicited admissions about self-limitations on a daily basis. My wife, Lisa, and I will walk through a grocery store or sit at a restaurant with our six children and, without fail, people will ask if they are all ours. After hearing the answer, they will almost inevitably say, "I could never do that." They often go on to say that they love big families because they were raised in one, but that they could never see themselves having a big family of their own.

I can relate. I said the same things before I had six children! I was very much against having a large family. I was motivated partially by selfishness: I despised the idea of being trapped into the responsibility of taking care of children for the rest of my life. I wanted to get it done while I was young and then be free of that responsibility and expense. Looking back, I can't believe how shallow that sounds, but it's true. I felt that way. But not all of my motivation was greed. I also felt as though it would be impossible to give more than three children the attention and love they deserved. But an amazing thing happened, and through God's grace both my wife and I had a change of heart.

After having our first child, I felt like I was at maximum capacity for love. I wondered how I would have the capacity to love another child as much as the first. But then we had our second, and it happened. The love was there. My heart was made larger. My capacity grew, and the experience began allowing me to see that my potential for love was well beyond anything I had imagined. I used to say that I could never handle more than three children. That resignation began manifesting itself into never *wanting* more than three children.

With each additional child, my capacity for love increased. To this day, I wonder how much love I am capable of. Although I love imperfectly, I do love more than I ever thought I could. And my ability to have a close relationship with each of the children is as great as it was when we only had one.

What I did not realize at the time was that I was confusing my *capacity* with my *potential*. Right now, you may be doing the same thing. For example, you may think you've reached your top earning potential, so instead of pursuing further education, learning new skills, or performing better in your job, you rest on your false belief that you've gone as far as you're going to go. But chances are very good that with some work and dedication, you could get promoted at work or find a new job altogether, even one that better matches your skill set and passion. The point is that it's easy to underestimate your current capacity, which in turn limits your overall potential.

This is exactly the opposite of what it means to win the world. Winning the world means maximizing your current capacity so that, in the long run, you can maximize your overall potential. Remember, winning the world simply means being the person you are meant to be and living the life you are meant to live. You can start today by tapping into your existing capacity and dedicating yourself to developing your maximum potential. There's no one else like you in the universe, so it's imperative to be the best you possible.

Winning Questions

1. Name two areas of your life where you can imagine getting better over time. What is your basis for thinking you have potential for growth in these areas? (For example, you have grown in the past; others have commented on your skill level; a colleague expressed confidence in your ability.)

2. What assumptions have you made about your ability *right now* in these areas? In other words, how do you view your present *capacity?*

3. For ten minutes, imagine what might happen if your assessment of your capacity is too low. What if you

already have the ability to do some of the things you wish to do? How would this affect your plans for the short run? Your understanding of yourself?

4. Now, map out what it might look like to dedicate yourself to reaching your maximum potential. What changes would you make in your attitude and behavior? What would you keep the same? What would a six-month plan look like? Twelve months?

Chapter Three

AVOID SHORT-TERM GRATIFICATION TRAPS

W INNING THE WORLD depends on exercising self-control and self-discipline. When we desire immediate gratification, we compromise both of these essential practices. It's easy to fall into short-term gratification traps without even realizing what's happening. This chapter shines a light on the pathway to winning the world in order to help you avoid short-term gratification traps that knock you off course and keep you from your ultimate goals.

Everyone has obligations, many of which we do not choose for ourselves. In the United States we are obligated to follow the law, pay taxes, and remain loyal to our country. Throughout history, many Americans have been obligated to defend the country in battle. These are the laws of our land, like it or not.

The obligation to maximize your potential is also one you did not choose, but it exists anyway. That obligation is not subject to the laws of the land; however, it is subject to the natural law and the laws of nature. In simple terms, the natural law is based on the structure of reality itself and is an unchanging rule or pattern. In other words, natural law is not made by human beings, but all human beings are capable of discovering it and living by it. Natural law guides you to choose good over evil even if, in the short term, it seems to be against your own self-interest. Disciplines such as philosophy and theology work to understand what natural law is and how it relates to human life.

Likewise, the laws of nature guide the natural world and are described by such disciplines as physics and biology. The penalties for breaking these laws are different from the penalties for breaking the laws of government. If you break a national or state law, you can be fined or imprisoned, but if you break the natural law or the laws of nature, you will interfere with your ability to thrive and grow. You may become sick, confused, guilt-ridden, or depressed.

At first glance, it may not seem like pursuing immediate gratification violates these natural laws. But every time we make a decision that violates our values or hurts someone else simply to serve our own need for instant gratification, we compromise our ability to reach our full potential.

Most poor decisions are made for the purpose of immediate gratification, and there are countless opportunities to choose short-term gratification over long-term gratification, such as:

1. Spending money you don't have on things you don't need

2. Sleeping in when you should get up

3. Eating a second piece of pie when you know you've already eaten too much, watching television when you should be playing with the kids or doing the dishes, or cutting corners at work

The outcome of serving your need for immediate gratification always includes dissatisfaction. In some cases, the dissatisfaction can be a minor sense of guilt or inconvenience or a little extra work. On weightier matters, the dissatisfaction can be painful.

While it might sound like something familiar to you from contemporary psychology or motivational books, the struggle between short- and long-term gratification is as old as the human race. Philosophers such as Socrates, Plato, Aristotle, Augustine, and Thomas Aquinas examined these human desires. Even contemporary educators such as Robert Spitzer continue to teach based on these ancient philosophies.

If I may be so bold, I am going to stir some of their ideas into one big casserole in order to apply them to our topic of winning the world. I recognize that I risk oversimplifying the intellectual splendor of these great thinkers. But their core insights offer some crucial resources for our goal of winning the world.

Joy and Happiness

We were all made with a desire for joy. Almost everything we do, we do to achieve joy. The problem is that many people confuse joy with its close relative, happiness. That confusion can lead to falling into the short-term gratification trap. You might think I am splitting hairs with these two words, but there is great value in the distinction.

The road to joy is paved with dedication, and the road to happiness is paved with "fun." Therefore, many of us will take the shorter path to happiness. Happiness wears off as soon as the source of our happiness is consumed, discarded, or ended. In other words, happiness goes away after the positive *feelings* associated with it dissolve. Joy, on the other hand, continues even in the midst of pain and suffering. That is why a mother would describe childbirth as very painful but simultaneously joyful. But very few women would ever describe their hours of labor as a *happy* time!

Unfortunately, people sometimes mistakenly believe that the path to happiness is the same as the road to joy, when in reality the former relates to the moment while the latter relates to a long-term state, a way of being. Seeking happiness alone and treating it as an end in itself can even lead to emptiness and unhappiness. For example, the desire for happiness in the moment can motivate a man to have an affair, while the desire for joy is what motivates him to remain faithful to his wife. The desire for happiness can motivate you to tell a lie; the desire for joy can motivate you to tell the truth regardless of the outcome. With happiness in mind, you'll eat an entire pan of brownies. If your eye is on joy, you'll eat in moderation.

I'm not trying to paint happiness as completely bad. It *is* good in the right perspective. Eating a candy bar, which can bring only happiness, not joy, is good as long as you only expect to get happiness from it. When expectation does not meet reality, however, people feel empty — "I thought I'd be happy now, but I'm not." To prevent dissatisfaction and even emptiness, it's important to match your expectations with the level of gratification actually experienced from activities, accomplishments, relationships, or attitudes.

As we move more deeply into how to win the world without losing our souls, we'll examine three primary sources of short-term gratification:

1. Physical gratification

2. Accomplishment gratification

3. Philanthropic gratification

Physical Gratification

Physical gratification is the most enticing and usually the most immediate of the short-term gratification traps. The human desire for joy may appear to be satisfied by short-term physical gratification, but in reality it is at best a form of temporary happiness.

Physical gratification is not a bad thing. The desire to eat something because it tastes delicious is good in proper measure. However, if you eat to find joy, you'll never stop eating because joy can't be found in food. Instead of finding joy, you'll gain weight, lose energy, and, depending on how far it goes, possibly suffer a heart attack or other diet-related illness.

When people seek joy in food, they find only fleeting happiness, which disappears as soon as the food is consumed. In order to make happiness feel like joy, which is in essence long-lasting, they need to string food together in a "chain of happiness." Every time they come down from the pleasure of the last thing they ate, they eat again. Of course, when you overeat, the law of nature kicks in with respect to your body. A happiness chain made up of Hershey bars is obviously going to take a toll on a person's waistline and glucose levels. The same holds true with excessive smoking and drinking, which begin to damage the lungs, liver, and skin.

There is also an *emotional* consequence that comes from trying to find joy in physical gratification. Making the deliberate decision to ignore your conscience by eating too much will cause guilt. That guilt is produced by failing to follow the natural order of things, which orients your innate sense of right and wrong. Your innate grasp of the natural law protects you from yourself, reminding you that you know very well you shouldn't be doing what you're doing.

I'll never forget talking to a young businessman who moved from his hometown in rural Wisconsin to downtown Chicago. He told me that he went from living a chaste life to sleeping around every weekend. He said that at first it was difficult because his conscience told him it was wrong to use women simply as objects for his own pleasure. But he went on to say that after a while his conscience slowly disappeared, and now he just does what he wants without worrying about it.

Think back to your earliest days when you took something you knew was not yours, said something that hurt someone's feelings, or took advantage of another person. You felt *guilty*. Your conscience spoke to you and, as a result, you later avoided that behavior and found joy, or you ignored your conscience in pursuit of short-term gratification. The more you ignore your conscience, the more you weaken its ability to influence your behavior until it finally enters an almost comatose state.

Once your conscience falls asleep, you become more susceptible to short-term gratification traps and you move farther away from winning the world. In the example of overeating, the result is sickness or weight gain. When it comes to promiscuity, the penalty can be catching a disease, crushing people's emotions, and (if you are a woman) getting pregnant or (if you are a man) causing someone you don't truly care about to become pregnant. If you steal, you risk jail time, and you undermine your ability to value what belongs to others, as well as the ability of others to trust you. The more active your conscience is, the less your odds are of engaging in risky behavior, and the higher they are of winning the world.

So when it comes to overeating, you either heed the warning that your conscience is giving you by curtailing consumption, or you beat that warning down and pursue the immediate gratification. If you do the latter, the result is physical and emotional pain. The physical pain is the result of breaking a law of nature, and the emotional pain is a result of breaking the natural law.

The physical and emotional pain must be healed by turning away from the habit. Failing to do this will result in increasing the volume and frequency of your consumption in order to mask both forms of pain. Increased consumption is always the mechanism used to compensate for the lack of pleasure that comes from previous portions. This is true about all forms of immediate physical gratification.

Drug addicts are the first to recognize this. Teenagers who get "high" off a nicotine buzz later need more quantity and frequency to get the same thrill. They may move to pot to satisfy their high. At some point, they may snap out of the pattern, recognizing the potential danger of the path they have chosen. Or they will "experiment" with even harder drugs, such as cocaine, crystal meth, or heroin.

Probably the most obvious form of immediate gratification in our society comes from sex. Sex addiction is now among the most common addictions that rehab centers deal with. Millions of people search for joy by having sex. In fact, you may remember the book with that suggestion as its very title.

No doubt, sex can be a part of a joyful experience between a man and a woman, but natural law demonstrates that anything used for what it was not intended for does not lead to joy. So a married man who has sex with anyone other than his wife will never find joy. He may find physical gratification and call it happiness, and, like the person who keeps eating candy bars, he might string together one sex partner after another to keep getting his fix of pleasure, but as soon as the act itself is over, he will feel remorse unless he has completely weakened his conscience. Eventually his behavior will lead to divorce or, at the least, total dissatisfaction with his wife. No matter what she's like, she will no longer be enough to feed his sexual appetite. Emptiness is an inevitable outcome in such a circumstance.

Every infraction against the natural law causes pain, even if it isn't felt immediately. A thief may get away with stealing for years. He may evade the police, but he will always live as a fugitive, even if he's the only one who knows. Even if he warps his conscience to the degree that he no longer cares about his crimes from a moral point of view, he will still live in the paranoia that he might get caught. He will be in a mental prison even if he is physically free.

It is of course impossible to maximize your potential if you are fixated on immediate gratification at a physical level. Self-control, self-mastery, and self-discipline are all required to counter these desires. These are characteristics of people who move to the next level of gratification.

Accomplishment Gratification

Some people go from one form of gratification to another in a single day, but most often people spend the majority of their time fixated on one type.

The pursuit of accomplishment gratification is often what replaces the quest for immediate physical gratification. Time and time again, talk shows feature success stories about people who lost substantial weight. Their stories usually include the confessions about their disordered relationship with food. They admit seeking happiness in a cheeseburger or chocolate cake.

After reaching rock bottom emotionally and physically, some people turn things around and successfully lose the weight. The feeling that they get from accomplishing such a goal becomes a new sense of happiness for them. They graduate from physical gratification, which came from food, to accomplishment gratification, which comes from reaching goals.

Examples of graduating from one level to the next go well beyond losing weight. There are countless people who have been liberated from a life of other addictions, such as drugs and sex. Many people whose addictions prevented them from productivity have gone on to become gainfully employed and highly successful. Obviously, this demonstrates that seeking gratification from accomplishment is a good thing. In fact it is part of winning the world.

It is important to remember that all people can and should graduate from one level to the next. I have coached clients who have earned huge sums of money but had nothing to show for it due to sloppy spending habits. On the outside they looked like they had it together. Even their private lives were free from most vices — with the exception of financial discipline. Their laziness with money stemmed from a desire to live easy in the moment. But by graduating from physical gratification (the ease of the moment), they reached impressive savings goals.

You'll find great satisfaction in accomplishing things that you have been gifted to do. That satisfaction is motivating and will drive you to continue to get results. If you expect that feeling of gratification to make you happy, then you will probably experience a long string of gratifications from your work. If, on the other hand, you expect it to make you *joyful*, you'll probably become dissatisfied. The expectation that accomplishment can cause joy rather than happiness is one of the reasons that, now more than ever, people change jobs and careers several times. Sometimes this stems from financial necessity, but more often it's the result of unrealistic expectations. They are looking for joy from something that, no matter how good it is, can never give joy.

When most people pursue destructive physical gratification, they have critics. People tell them to straighten up and get their act together. Outside pressure sometimes even rekindles their conscience. Accomplishment, however, is met with a different reaction. People tell you that they are proud of you, or they give you a bonus check for your results. They tell you to keep up the good work, which encourages your performance.

These outcomes are good, except that they can shift the source of happiness from living with purpose to recognition or rewards. I have witnessed many people become recognition addicts. They thirst for the spotlight, "attaboy!" and a bonus check. But after a while they need a louder "attaboy" and a bigger check in order to get the same high. This is the type of thing that can motivate athletes to use performance-enhancing drugs. The huge list of guilty athletes, ranging from baseball's José Canseco to Olympic stars like Marion Jones, only represents a larger problem that trickles all the way down into high school sports.

If accomplishment is pursued in order to find joy, then the chain of happiness present in physical gratification will repeat itself, only with gold medals in place of Hershey bars. Such people will need to accomplish loftier goals, grander objectives, or more frequent payouts in order to simulate joy.

They can eventually become disenchanted, like professional athletes who have called $50 million contracts "insulting" because another athlete signed one for $60 million. When a $50 million paycheck is anything but good news, you know you have a problem! That attitude comes from expecting joy as a result of accomplishment. Even if the athlete got paid $100 million, he would not be joyful. He might be happy for a moment, but that won't last.

Walk down Wall Street or Hollywood Boulevard, or watch ESPN, and you will see living proof of people who seem to have it all but in reality are not joyful. You will find lots of rich, accomplished, powerful, and *miserable* people. If, like them, you get caught up in a hardcore habit of striving for success as an end in itself, you can warp your conscience and break the natural law. Your desire to accomplish may become so paramount that anyone or anything that gets in your way must be removed or run over. Things can become more important than people, and self-centeredness can be considered a virtue.

Your accomplishments may be righteous, like getting better grades, raising more respectful children, helping others, or earning more money. All of these can be re-minders that you are living with purpose. If you expect *happiness* from your accomplishments, you will surely gain it. If you expect more, you may risk losing every-thing. As we will see in later chapters, winning the world is about avoiding short-term gratification traps and focus-ing on long-term gratification. True freedom, true success, means being disciplined about putting your individual ac-complishments into a broader context of the person you want to be. In the end, winning the world is about defin-ing success, knowing when enough is enough, caring for your neighbor, and being grateful for who you are and what you have.

Philanthropic Gratification

As we've discussed, if you search for your joy in physical gratification, it's only a matter of time before you discover that you can't eat enough, smoke enough, or have sex enough to find joy. Inspired by that fact, you may seek joy in accomplishment, only to realize that you can't win enough, earn enough, or get enough recognition to be joyful. Still hungry for joy, many people have committed themselves to philanthropy. They assume that joy will certainly come from something as good as giving, so they whip out their wallets, feed the poor, and travel to impoverished nations to distribute medicines.

Famous billionaires have gotten publicity for making the leap from accomplishment gratification to philanthropic gratification. There is the well-publicized story of Warren Buffet giving his billions to the Gates family foundation to be used for philanthropy as they see fit. Other well-known billionaires such as Ted Turner, George Soros, and Tom Monaghan have also given away money by the bucketsful.

These big names sometimes stir up debate by choosing controversial beneficiaries, but most people don't debate that being generous with money can be good if the cause is worthy. After finding emptiness from physical consumption and accomplishment consumption, many wealthy people soften their hearts and "give back," and at first it feels good. But if they aren't mindful, the same dangerous pattern can ensue. Ted Turner, for example, has publicly shared his personal grief and unhappiness despite giving away hundreds of millions. On the other hand,

Tom Monaghan appears to have peace as he gives because his purpose goes well beyond giving just to feel good. Mr. Monaghan, the founder of Dominoes Pizza, gives to causes that support his Catholic beliefs and sees these efforts as part of getting to Heaven. The tricky part for many givers is that the happiness that comes from donating large sums of money may resemble joy, but it's still only happiness.

Soon the feeling goes away. Then, in order to regain the feeling, the benefactors must give more or increase the frequency of their giving. Eventually, they build artificial joy in the form of a charitable chain of happiness.

Countless people who set out to serve the poor and care for the sick get burned out. Of course, it is possible to suffer from physical exhaustion, but I'm referring to being burnt out mentally or emotionally. They set out to give for self-serving purposes, seeking their own rewards such as accolades from others for being so good and so generous. But the chain of happiness is exhausting, and it never ends in joy.

Still others live an entire life of service with the same zeal in their last days as they had when they started. Mother Teresa is probably the world's best-known example. She served the poor tirelessly and never slowed down. She did not seek anything for herself, not even emotions such as happiness. To her, giving was an act of emptying herself. It was a part of living with purpose by honoring God through service. I have no doubt that her selfless attitude produced both happiness and joy, but only as a byproduct of natural law. She followed her conscience and strove to serve as she was created to serve. Her recently released writings talk of the darkness and pain she felt, but she pressed forward anyway, realizing that long-term joy is always sweeter than fleeting happiness.

The attitude of service she had was mission-oriented. When developing an organizational culture, leaders can glean something from Mother Teresa's approach. The more the culture of an organization is centered on the mission, the greater the employee retention will be. The more compelling the mission, the more employees overlook their personal dissatisfactions. They go from being motivated by personal happiness to being motivated by a cause. A cause is always bigger than an individual, which means that it is more common to have people become selfless in the pursuit.

Philanthropic gratification is the longest lasting of the short-term gratification motivators because it is often selfless in nature. A giving person is often predisposed to finding long-term gratification, which is required if you want to win the world.

Winning Questions

1. Take a moment to think about your current life. Where might you be experiencing pleasure but falling prey to a short-term gratification trap? Where are you seeking physical gratification? Are your goals here to find joy and meaning or to find happiness? Are you content with where you are physically? Do you expect joy where you can find only happiness? If there are ways that you take a "Hershey bar" approach to your physical gratification, how might you learn

not to seek gratification in those ways? What support would you need to make such a change?

2. Where are you seeking accomplishment gratification? Are you addicted to getting ahead and being recognized for everything you do? Do you work in a competitive, money-driven environment that entices you to do "whatever it takes" to reach your benchmarks and earn your bonus? Do you find it difficult to know when enough is enough? While accomplishment is a good thing on the path to winning the world, is your desire to be accomplished an end in itself? Take a moment to assess your overall definition of success and how your accomplishments fit into that larger horizon. What do you notice? What might you change to move from short-term gratification to long-term gratification?

3. Identify areas in your life where you have or would like to have accomplishment and philanthropic gratification. Are your motives for this more about the good for the other person or what the achievements and giving would say about you?

4. Are there any areas of life where you feel that your conscience has been silenced by too much behavior that contradicts the natural law? How could you start to strengthen your conscience and let it be heard clearly again?

∽ Chapter Four ∝

EMBRACE LONG-TERM GRATIFICATION

Existential Gratification

EXISTENTIAL GRATIFICATION is the peace and fulfill-
ment that come with knowing that you're living
with a purpose and *for* a purpose. To understand what
this means, let's consider some key concepts from major
thinkers. Steven Covey describes a concept similar to existential gratification in his runaway bestseller *The 7 Habits
of Highly Effective People.* Habit #2 is: "Begin with the
end in mind." Covey says, "Although Habit 2 applies to
many different circumstances and levels of life, the most
fundamental application of 'begin with the end in mind'
is to begin today with the image, picture, or paradigm of
the end of your life as your frame of reference or criterion
by which everything else is examined."

In *Man's Search for Meaning,* Jewish psychologist Victor Frankl describes logotherapy, which is a type of
therapy he developed as a result of witnessing the behavior of his fellow prisoners in Nazi concentration camps.
He noticed that those prisoners, like himself, who had an
extended outlook fared better than prisoners who could
not see past the present. Those who were not crushed by

the fear of captivity and extermination hoped as far out into the future as possible. They considered the "exit." The foundation of Frankl's therapy is to help people realize that life has meaning under all circumstances, even the most miserable ones; we have freedom to find meaning in what we do and experience. Taken to its fullest, a person who hopes as far out as possible deals with the question, "Why am I here, and what will happen to me when I die?" Everyone grapples with that question at some point in life. The sooner you find answers, the sooner you feel true joy.

Emmy Award–winner Fulton Sheen talked about "existential neurosis," which is basically the mental confusion that anyone will experience if he neglects thinking about his purpose, outcomes, or origins. Sheen shares the story of a missionary who was traveling with a guide through the mountains of Tibet during a snowstorm. The missionary heard a man beg for help after he'd fallen down a crevasse and was trapped alone. The missionary begged the guide to help him save the man's life. The guide refused, claiming that they would all freeze to death if they took the time. The missionary refused to leave the man and decided to help while the guide went on to camp alone.

He found the stranger and carried him safely to the camp, but when they arrived the guide was not there. He had frozen to death before he arrived. Sheen points out that the missionary saw the big picture and was motivated by his ability to step outside of himself. The motivation found from the mission to save the stranger may have been what saved the missionary's life. It gave him purpose and a clear picture of his desired outcome.

Living without considering the outcome of your actions or testing your belief systems eventually leads to dissatisfaction. Neglecting these fundamental responsibilities can cause intellectual confusion and flawed philosophies, which can affect the way you make decisions at work, at home, and in social settings.

That is the main point behind Covey's second habit, which is a concept that had been preached in the workplace for centuries even before he wrote about it. If you don't stop to consider the result of your actions, you'll flail around in all of your roles. The cost of this is expensive no matter what you do. In parenting, it causes unruly children. And in the workplace, it's the source of waste and low productivity.

At some point in life, all of us have asked ourselves, "What am I doing here? What is my purpose?" This is why Rick Warren's book *The Purpose Driven Life* struck a chord and sold tens of millions of copies. Simply put, people want *meaning*. In the animated movie *A Bug's Life*, a fly at a circus is impatiently sitting in the stands waiting to be entertained. Finally, he gets up and yells, "I've only got twenty-four hours to live, and I ain't wasting it here!" If you only had twenty-four hours to live, how would you spend your time? What answers would you need to find?

A story illustrates this point. A group of four monks were playing cards when they heard the news that the world was going to end in one hour. Immediately the first monk got up to phone his brother to ask for forgiveness. The second ran to his mother and told her he loved her. The third gave away a small stash of money he had been hiding under his mattress. The fourth stayed and dealt himself a hand of solitaire. He had no need to run around at the last minute because he'd already taken care of business in preparation for this day.

He was the only monk who was playing cards with a clear conscience. He had considered the outcome of his previous actions and reconciled them. He had been experiencing existential gratification.

When you live with a guilty conscience, whether because of something you did or something you failed to do, you won't experience joy. You may even begin to run from your conscience by deceiving yourself. This can rock the foundations of logic within your mind and affect unrelated aspects of it.

When you live with internal peace, you have a tendency to treat others around you better and think more clearly. I witness this when I consult with entrepreneurs. When they are under heavy financial stress, they often are short-tempered with clients, employees, and even relatives. (And they *know* they are being short.) The point is that stress from one source, in this case financial strain, can affect things that are closely related, such as employees. But it also affects things that are more indirectly related, such as family.

One of the greatest stories of how one man's short-term thinking affected many people is that of King David. He snuck a look at Bathsheba, a married woman, while she was bathing in the nude, and he became filled with lust.

He called her into his presence, and then he slept with her and she became pregnant. Instead of facing the truth, he called home her husband, Uriah, who was serving as a loyal soldier in David's army. David hoped that Bathsheba and her husband would join together while Uriah was home so that David wouldn't be discovered as the father. David's plan failed because Uriah was so loyal that, in accordance with military custom, he returned to the battlefield without sleeping with Bathsheba.

David might have faced the truth at this stage, but he didn't. Instead, he gave orders to have Uriah sent to the front lines, hoping that he would be killed in battle. His plan worked, but he was riddled with guilt. His initial mistake caused a series of bad decisions. Instead of leading a nation, David spent time figuring out how to cover his tracks. His distraction even affected his military decisions.

The point is that when the closet of your conscience is untidy, you will do lots of crazy things to prevent others from opening it. People who are not at ease with the basic question of "why am I here and what is my purpose?" sometimes act like King David. They act irrationally and selfishly hope that the outcome of their actions will lead to satisfaction, but it never does.

Such people often adopt false philosophies in life in order to make up for their emptiness. Sometimes believing in false philosophies is a way for them to justify certain behaviors. At some point all of us have desired to believe something that was not true because adhering to the truth might mean being embarrassed or realizing that we must change our behaviors.

Existential gratification can't truly exist without coming to grips with the fact that you did not create you. It is about exploring with a sincere heart and clear mind how you got to be here in the first place. That question invites the follow-up question: "Where will I go after I die?" At a certain point all people grapple with this concept, which is why they can categorize themselves as Christian, Jew, Muslim, New Ager, Hindu, Buddhist, agnostic, or atheist.

Adhering to any of these philosophies means that you accept the basis of my point. You have considered the source of your existence, and that consideration is why you categorize yourself as one of the above. But how seriously have you considered it? People who find peace — that is, existential gratification — test their philosophies and do not fear dialogue about conflicting ideas.

One way to recognize people who have not reached the level of existential gratification is by their defensiveness: they don't want to talk about it, because they know at some level that their beliefs are weak and really can't withstand much conversation. Another sign is when someone claims that discussing the idea of origins and outcomes is merely a ploy to impose a religious ideology. This idea is false because, in fairness, people could use the same discussion to advance their agnostic or atheistic views as well.

I once had a conversation about existential matters with a well-educated and intelligent man whom I admire. He was an agnostic primarily because (as he said) violent attempts to advance religion are responsible for more deaths than any other man-made cause. He cited the Crusades, *jihad,* and witch hunts, to name a few. While I don't share his agnosticism, his passionate interest in these questions reminded me that existential questions apply to all of us, and all of us will suffer if we are afraid to address them frankly. And in our conversation, where I reminded him of the over 100 million people who had died in secular wars and attempts to *rid* the world of religion (such as the deaths under Stalin), we were both able to investigate our beliefs so that we could comfortably, intellectually, and honestly defend them as true or reject them in favor of what is true.

Most of us grapple with other long-term, end-in-mind decisions. We press on for new information to determine if our old philosophies are true or flawed. We wrestle with questions like, how can I best save for retirement? The better our foundational philosophies are, the greater our long-term wealth will be.

In a similar vein, if an architect designs a skyscraper with a fundamental flaw located in the footings of the building, then the entire building is compromised. It takes a firm foundation to build anything to its greatest heights. So if you are living with basic philosophies that are flawed, then other, seemingly unrelated beliefs may contain errors as well. What would happen if you simply replaced one simple truth in the mind of the most brilliant engineer? What if he believed that $3 + 1$ equaled 5? Even if it were his only error, it would render virtually everything that he created useless.

The founding fathers of the United States of America knew that they needed to establish a government with the furthest vision of the future as possible. They never believed that America would live on eternally, but they wrote documents to protect it for as long as possible. In a way, their groundwork was an existential outlook for a nation. This inspired them to establish laws that mirrored the natural law, knowing that this would contribute to the greatest chance of success. They argued, debated, and wrestled with ideas. The first several paragraphs in the Declaration of Independence illuminate their conclusions. Consider these remarkable words:

> When in the Course of human events, it becomes necessary for one people to dissolve the political bands which have connected them with another, and to assume among the powers of the earth, the separate and equal station to which the Laws of Nature and of Nature's God entitle them, a decent respect to the opinions of mankind requires that they should declare the causes which impel them to the separation.
>
> We hold these truths to be self-evident, that all men are created equal, that they are endowed by their Creator with certain unalienable Rights, that among these are Life, Liberty and the pursuit of Happiness.

"Laws of Nature," "Nature's God," "self-evident truths," and "unalienable rights" are all phrases derived from natural law. Contrast those freedoms with the doctrines of Karl Marx's *Communist Manifesto*. The manifesto was based on the idea that capitalism was evil and that all forms of greed are a result of social class. That claim was an error, and it contradicted natural law because, among other things, human beings have a natural desire to choose for themselves what is in their best interest. It was not thought through by its inventors nor was it voluntarily tested. It was forced upon people, and it failed despite Herculean efforts made by its proponents.

Failing to consider the outcomes of your actions renders you less effective in life and reduces your ability to motivate yourself into action. People who don't think matters through are more defensive in nature because they are less secure. They either know that their philosophies are weak or, even if on an emotional level they believe they are strong, they cannot articulate them. This makes them agitated when people question them. It is what fuels their desire to force their philosophies on people through warfare, suppression, and mass murder. Think of Mussolini, Stalin, and Hitler — none of these people were ever described as happy, let alone joyful.

You must develop your own declaration and constitutions for living based on sound philosophy, not idealistic errors. If your beliefs about yourself are in error, then you will never reach your own potential.

A sincere discussion of these beliefs is ultimately the only path to sanity. I have not known anyone to have peace who does not consider his purpose, and I have not known anyone to have discovered his purpose without considering his origin. Understanding your purpose is a way to understand human nature at large. The more you understand human nature, the more you will be effective in the world. Teachers, leaders, parents, and decision makers avoid fundamental errors if they understand the basic needs of all people made known in the natural law.

How does all of this relate to winning the world? The further out we put our focus on long-term gratification, the more we will reach our own potential in life. This is an easy concept to witness on a daily basis. A child who refuses to take medicine because she desires to avoid an unpleasant short-term taste doesn't understand the outcome of her actions or the outcome of the medicine. An entrepreneur who quits during her first challenge may not be considering the outcome of her hard work. She ventured out and opened her own business to control her hours and pay and to make decisions freely, but at the first sign of trouble, she thinks only of the work or stress she faces today. She trades in the long-term gratification for the short-term stress relief.

To win the world, try to see things as far out as possible. Take the long view. Explore all outcomes with a sincere heart and a sharp intellect. Challenge yourself to crave delayed gratification and to suppress, to a reasonable degree, short-term gratification. Living that way sweetens everyday life.

Winning Questions

1. At this moment, how would you answer the question "Why am I here, and what will happen to me when I die?" Ask yourself as well who you are and how you got here.

2. Are these questions part of your daily life? Are you in the habit of thinking about them? If not, why not?

3. Take each question in turn and apply the answer (the answer you would currently give) to your current professional goals. How can each answer support what you are trying to do? How might each answer challenge you and lead you to ask other questions? Would you say you experience "existential gratification," or do you have some progress to make?

4. What changes do you need to make to live with purpose and meaning? To be truthful with yourself so that you can reach your full potential?

∂ Chapter Five ∂

RESOLVE IS MORE THAN
A POSITIVE ATTITUDE

WHEN I COACH entrepreneurs, I ask as many questions as I can before I provide solutions. I want to know how they perceive their current circumstance, whether it's good or bad. Did they earn their success? Did they inherit it? Were they lucky? Could they duplicate it? Are they succeeding or failing because of outside influences or because of their own ability or inability to get things done? Sometimes the answers entrepreneurs give demonstrate a keen awareness of strengths and weaknesses, and other times their answers are quite vague.

Some coaches never accept any answers from their clients that are not positive. They claim that all outcomes are in the control of the subject and that a positive attitude can change anything. I see why that approach is seductive, but there's one problem with it. It's patently false. Imagine if their client was a passenger on an airplane that was about to crash — how would a positive attitude change that? Sometimes business is very much like that airplane. For example, you might choose to buy a franchise only for the franchisor to go bankrupt six months later. In a situation like that, the last thing you need to hear from a coach is, "Just stay positive."

On the other hand, if your business is about to go belly-up from things outside your control, a negative attitude will not solve anything either. It's important to be realistic and focus on results rather than lamenting defeats. Once you realize that you can't change the past, you come to realize that your only choice is to impact the future. The same is true, of course, for parents, teachers, secretaries, and everyone else.

Poor results or the after-effects of defeats from outside influences can leave people jaded. They sometimes start to find reasons why they'll fail again and again. If you define success as proving to yourself and everyone around you that you'll fail, then you're guaranteed success, but only of the most absurd kind.

Fortunately, I've coached many people who have the opposite perspective. They look for all the reasons why they'll succeed. From the start, they ensure their success by determining the value of all their actions no matter how they fare. But they aren't pollyannaish about what it means to succeed. Unlike the limited positive attitude crowd or those who seek their own failure, they don't redefine success by lowering standards. Even when they fail, they assess the situation and move forward with their new knowledge and deeper understanding.

Armed with such resolve to succeed, they find practical, rational, and beneficial ways to guarantee success by looking for more than one potential outcome to most situations. In other words, they see the experiences as legitimate future buying power, and they plan on spending every dime. They know that every failure they experience will provide an insight into how to avoid the same situation down the road. Such practices don't make them passive, however. They never accept failure without a fight. And unlike the "positive attitude" folk, they call it like it is, which means that they acknowledge poor results and label them as such.

Why is this approach so crucial? Because once you start glossing over failure and pretending it wasn't really failure, you're training yourself to deny reality. And the next time you need to be savvy about a situation, you're going to have a harder time sizing up reality and acting effectively. So it turns out that "positive attitude" crowd, who always seem to bounce back when they face defeat, are really only paving the way to more defeat. On the other hand, people who sincerely fight to win know when they need to acknowledge defeat in order to ensure future victories. In other words, they don't just walk around with a positive attitude on the outside; they actually have resolve on the inside.

Resolve is what enables a soldier to be focused on the enemy's defeat while simultaneously remaining level-headed. It's what allows him to shed a tear for a fellow soldier while loading his weapon. Resolve looks completely different from a positive attitude. Thousands of positive attitude rallies are run every day at sales meetings across the country. Too often, they are run by managers who don't have answers for the specific challenges facing their sales teams. They mask their doubts with a lot of enthusiasm and demand a smile from all the participants. But the participants instinctively know that this is false.

Contrast this with what happens when a sales manager with resolve runs a meeting. It doesn't reek of insincerity because it has dimension and depth. The meeting sounds dissatisfied yet still steadfast. It is filled with the acknowledgment of defeat but never the smell of disease. It's a meeting that inspires people to face doubt and insecurity. It's a meeting of empowerment, not a meeting of "happiness." Managers with resolve show the reps how to clean out all the manure they have to deal with, not how to mask it with fragrance.

When you become committed to winning the world, you must be real and stay grounded in the real world. You can't look at a picture of Mr. Olympia or Ms. America and repeat ten times a day "I will lose weight" and expect it to work. You must mentally prepare for battle and acknowledge that you will take enemy fire from self-doubt and everyday distractions.

In the case of losing weight, you must have the type of resolve that allows you to see things for what they are. You might identify weaknesses about yourself that a positive attitude disciple would never admit. If you recognize a poor track record of consistency for working out, then don't overestimate your willpower. Instead of being *positive*, be *practical*. Ensure your success by finding a workout partner. If that's not enough, hire a personal trainer, and be sure he charges you whether or not you show up. That might get you off the sofa.

Resolve is smarter than a positive attitude. A positive attitude tells you that you're fine the way you are. Resolve inspires you to change, and constant change is necessary if you are going to win the world. Pray for the grace to overcome weaknesses and recommit to your cause every day. Instead of fearing only negative thoughts, as some would say, fear positive thoughts that cause self-deceit. Be real. Get resolve and win the world.

Winning Questions

1. What are three areas in your life where you've tried to "think positive" instead of digging deep down into the habit of resolve?

2. Did the positive thinking provide you with the staying power you desired?

3. Where did your impulse for thinking "positive" come from? (A self-help book, a TV show, something you read online, a friend, etc.)

4. In what ways can positive thinking lead you to ignore important information you might need for real success?

5. What is your favorite example of someone who showed great resolve and ended up succeeding?

6. Following the advice in this chapter, what are three ways you could shift from "positive" thinking to *resolve*?

7. How will your new resolve help you attain your goals and win the world?

❧ *Chapter Six* ❧

BECOME A DIPLOMAT BETWEEN YOUR EMOTION AND LOGIC

A KEY FACTOR in your ability to win the world without losing your soul is how well you can navigate between emotions and logic, so that you remain grounded in reality.

As a matter of national security, diplomacy is the best way to prevent war, and it takes discipline and skill. The same is true in order to maintain peace in your own mind. Winning the world means being able to use intellectual diplomacy to prevent, lessen, or end the personal war being fought between the best and worst versions of yourself.

Your internal diplomat is the part of your brain designed to form rational and moral outcomes compelling enough to motivate you into action. It's the part of your brain that says, "I know what I must do. I know that I can do it. I know that I will do it." Knowledge is not always enough for you to get things done, but it's an important first step. Without it, nothing else works. Diplomacy is a combination of knowledge and self-control. Working together, these tools enable you to win battles of conscience that take place over both the important and the most mundane issues in life. Diplomacy puts your knowledge in motion.

Internal wars can loom ahead if you fail to respond properly to things such as self-doubt and unguarded emotions. Your emotions line up like missiles aimed at your logic. For example, you know that you should keep your emotions under wraps over an issue at work, but you just can't help yourself. Your co-worker is driving you crazy. You want to yell at him, but before you do, you enter into diplomatic discussions with yourself. If you succeed, then you communicate in an effective way, winning your co-worker over and obtaining a victory. If you fail, you start a firestorm of unnecessary bickering that has little to do with the objectives of your job.

Effective diplomats are known for their ability to defuse tensions by laying out logical solutions. They keep their cool even with missiles aimed right at them. For diplomacy to work, it must be based on sound philosophies and steady dialogue. You must develop logic so powerful that it overpowers emotion.

Logic is a philosophical discipline by which one systematically examines reality and seeks the truth. Everyone has a desire to know the truth. Many people, however, lose their yearning for the truth through years of disappointment, rejection, and taking shortcuts. As a result, they become skilled at self-deception, which eventually defeats reason and logic.

As they lose their taste for truth, it's common for people to silence their inner diplomat. If you do that, you'll replace your internal diplomat with internal deception, which results in intentionally hiding from the truth. This is never a pleasant thing to observe in others, but it is excruciating to discover in your own life. You deceive yourself because the pain associated with the truth hurts more than the pain of self-deception. Many people would rather hear a lie than the truth, if the truth hurts.

That includes lying to themselves. I remember the story of a group of friends who became irritated by the arrogance of one of them when it came to wine. His pretentiousness about all the "varietals" and "bouquets" and "clarity" inspired them to swap the labels on two bottles of wine — one very expensive and the other very cheap. Then, without telling him what they'd done, they casually asked his opinion of the two wines. Their friend failed the test miserably. He praised the cheap wine and mocked the fine wine. In fact, he went so overboard that some of the pranksters didn't even want to expose him to the truth, because the embarrassment would be too hard to witness.

But they did tell him the truth. He made up several reasons why he knew he was right. It became quite awkward for everyone. He denied the situation vehemently until he ran out of fuel to defend his point. His emotions — his desire to cling to certain ideas about the wine and about himself — won the war over his logic.

The approach that he took to defend himself was similar to what happens in your body when you experience serious physical pain. Your body sends natural painkillers to the source of unmanageable physical pain in order for you to deal with the situation in the short term. These natural drugs in your body are involuntary, so after a while they wear off. From that point on, your pain is managed by your will or by artificial drugs designed to simulate the natural chemicals in your body.

When you deceive yourself, a similar thing happens. The reaction is often involuntary. Your immediate response to making a mistake might be, "no way!" just like the phony wine snob. But if you have self-control, you may be able to prevent your internal response from becoming external. That opportunity buys you enough time to face the truth and accept the short-term pain in order to grow in the long run. If you choose to throw away that opportunity and succumb to the drug of self-deceit, you may become addicted to it. Soon your philosophies can become worthless because they will be devoid of reality, truth, and causality. The more you defend what you know to be false, the more you get hooked on the drug of self-deception. The longer this goes on, the more you lose your ability to reason and start to believe your own lies.

The definition of philosophy is the examination of truth, existence, reality, causality, and freedom. Each of these elements is related. You can't have truth without the knowledge of your existence, and you can't have freedom if you don't know what causes it. If you're going to win the war against yourself, you must be grounded in solid philosophy, one that commits you to facing reality honestly. Good philosophy will provide you with all the reasons to do what is right with your life and your skills. It's a building block for maximizing your potential and an insulator from self-deception.

Even if you have sound philosophies and you effectively negotiate your freedom, there is no guarantee that the enemy will not at least show his teeth. He will continue to build up arms across the border. The more your pride feels threatened by the truth, the greater the attacks will be. When your pride shows itself in the form of self-doubt, you can become capable of derailing even your best diplomatic efforts. Soon the rockets of unguarded emotion will launch. Why all this battle? Because nobody wants to be wrong, make mistakes, or look incompetent.

Your right hemisphere is the side of your brain that controls creativity and emotion. The left hemisphere controls the logical side. The right brain says, "Sex? Yeah, that sounds great!" and focuses on pleasure. The left brain always delays action until it answers the question, "What is the purpose of the thing I desire or am experiencing?" In the case of sex, the left brain may reason that sex is for unity and procreation between married couples. So which side wins the debate?

The frontal lobe helps settle the score by acting as the filter between the two. It helps bridge the gap between the left and right brain. It is what says, "Yeah, sex is pleasurable, and that is good, but it would be out of order if I pursue an affair to have sex." In other words, the frontal lobe is the diplomat that keeps you from making the big blunders in life. That ability is one of the most profound differences between human beings and animals. We have the ability to know the purpose of activities and make moral judgments about them.

If you're going to win the world, you must pursue the truth about yourself and your natural talents. You must know the truth about your skills and weaknesses in a manner that is free from the tyranny of your emotional right brain. If you let your right brain run free without reserve, you end up getting yourself in trouble.

Within reason, you must be willing to test your beliefs and convictions. If you fail to test your beliefs by examining your conscience, then you may live a lifetime of lies. For example, many years ago, a group of Japanese soldiers were found hiding on remote islands in the Philippines. They had deserted during World War II and, fearing the wrath of the emperor, stayed put for nearly forty years. You can imagine the regret they felt after hearing the news that the emperor had been defeated long ago and realizing they had wasted half their lives based on a false assumption.

Maybe you have a natural gift for the violin, but you got embarrassed after a huge mistake during a recital in the second grade. The embarrassment was so great that you convinced yourself you weren't capable of playing any instrument, so you quit. But what might have been if you'd stuck it out? Might you have become a virtuoso? This is a decision you made for life, and right or wrong, you made it with the immaturity of a seven-year-old.

Would anyone ask a seven-year-old for career advice? Of course not. But this is, in effect, what many of us have done for ourselves. We have made decisions about who we are and what we are capable of based on past experiences that may not have told the entire story. No doubt, some of these experiences do reveal some truth about our gifts, but others do not. It takes maturity to distinguish between the two.

If you're going to win the world, you must have an accurate understanding of your strengths, weaknesses, and potential. The only way to pull this off is by managing your emotions, adopting sound philosophy, and being humble. The greatest definition of humility I have ever heard is, "precision truth about who you are, good and bad." If we all had that type of humility, there would be no internal war, and your diplomat could take a much-deserved vacation.

Winning Questions

1. What are three recent events where, in the workplace or at home, you found your emotions trying to get the better of you?

2. Did your inner diplomat play any role in helping you negotiate between your emotions and your logical sense of the situation?

3. How good are you at letting your diplomat speak in stressful situations like those you listed? What are three ways you can let your diplomat's advice trump what your emotions are asking you to do?

4. What is the number-one area in your life right now where you feel detached from the truth of your life and afraid to make an honest assessment? (Examples: personal life, reputation in the office, work with colleagues.) Name two specific actions you can take to start assessing yourself more clearly.

5. How do you define winning the world? How can your inner diplomat help you keep your focus on the larger plan in your life so that you can attain your goals?

❧ *Chapter Seven* ❦

UNLEASH YOUR TALENT THROUGH SKILL AND INTENSITY

BOBBY FISCHER AMAZED people when, in 1958, he earned the title of grandmaster chess player at the age of fifteen. His success inspired many theories about what happens in the minds of intellectual super-achievers. How do successful people become successful? Researchers and pretty much anyone who had had a hand in developing talent, such as teachers, business leaders, and coaches, all offered opinions on the topic.

One of the popular opinions was that people like Bobby Fischer are simply endowed with a natural gift. They hit the lottery of talent simply by being born the way they were. This view obviously has some merit: we all know people who have taken to certain activities with initial ease.

Others surmised that great athletes, business leaders, and even chess players can see the future to some degree. That is, they see the next four or five plays ahead of them. This is also partially true. People in business, athletics, and politics will make decisions based on their ability to mentally play out scenarios to their furthest possible conclusions. In the game of chess, it was assumed that the grandmasters have a unique ability to see several plays ahead. This was a gift they inherited, just as a "born" salesperson has the natural ability to close a sale. But other research suggests that these great minds are developed more than they are hatched.

Over the past few decades, performance studies have become intense. Our society is one that values results; therefore, many people are interested in how to manufacture a higher level of human performance. While it's possible to measure the results of top business leaders, teachers, or even athletes, several variables make it difficult to objectively even out the playing field. This is one of the reasons why studying what happens in the mind of a chess player is of particular interest.

The results of a chess match are not influenced by the weather, economic conditions, or teammate performance. Chess is chess, and chess players use their minds, not athletic prowess and coordination. What determines success during a match is found entirely between the ears of the players. So what happens in the minds of the Bobby Fischers of the world?

Contrary to what many people think, the grandmasters do not see several plays ahead. Instead, they see the play sitting right in front of them, but they see it with tremendous clarity. A novice might see a multitude of potential plays when staring at the positions of the pieces. Most of them are poor choices, and seeing them increases the odds of making a poor move. But a grandmaster sees only the best and fewest options because he taps into his massive reservoir of knowledge about the game. Therefore, the odds of his choosing poorly are very low.

So where does this knowledge come from? Was the grandmaster born with extra chess software right out of the factory? The answer is no. Although a chess player may have an inclination to process chess with greater ease than others when first being introduced to the game, he or she develops it through practice or, more precisely, through skill.

A grandmaster is not born; he develops. Herbert A. Simon of Carnegie Mellon University is known for his research on memory and the minds of experts. One of the concepts Simon coined was his own psychological law, "the ten-year rule." Through research he determined that most people who commit ten years of intense training to a given field can become experts, even if they didn't possess a natural inclination for the topic. (Obviously, there are exceptions and limitations, such as limited natural physical strength, which may preclude the most dedicated persons from becoming world-class weightlifters even if they are able to develop the right mental faculties for the task.)

Chess seems to confirm the ten-year rule. Many grandmasters have been shown to have about ten years of experience under their belts before they reach that level. If it seems impossible, looking at your own life, to imagine becoming an expert in something in ten years, you should remember that "ten years" is now something of a metaphor. Even in something as complex as chess, many can achieve great things even *sooner*.

It used to be that a young aspiring chess player had to wait for his father to come home to play, or he had to wait to play with his grandfather on weekends. Of course, once he entered tournaments, the frequency of his play would have increased since he had found friends with the same interest. But he still needed to be in the presence of someone who knew the game in order to practice. Therefore, it would take at least ten years to gather experience.

Today, however, a five-year-old can boot up a grandmaster player any time he wants to. Therefore, a child playing chess with a computer can gain the ten years of experience in a much shorter time. As a result, the number of child grandmasters has increased. Today's record-holder, Sergey Karjakin, earned his title at twelve years seven months. (In the August 2006 edition of *Scientific American*, Philip Ross develops the chess example in his well-written article "The Expert Mind.")

My father taught me this lesson inadvertently. Immediately upon my graduation from college, he told me the following. "Depending on how you handle your responsibilities, you'll look back on life in thirty years and determine that you've had one year of experience thirty times over. Or, if you're diligent, you can gain thirty years of experience in the next five years."

The experience gathered by repetition is more valuable than the natural talent one might possess at the moment of conception. In fact, my experience after training over a hundred thousand business professionals demonstrates that, in some regards, talent may serve as a factor for failing. The ideal formula for success is a naturally talented person who commits to developing his skills. In some cases, however, talented people can "win" while resting on their laurels. They may fail to train themselves, whereas a less talented person must rely on training in order to compete with talented people. The additional training builds "mental muscle," and that eventually can lead to a faster pace of learning.

One good thing about being born with talent is that early successes can often inspire motivation. A young, talented person may be recognized for her performance in school, on the sports field, or on stage. That recognition may fuel her desire to continue to develop her skills. If she continues, she is a prime candidate for great success. On the other hand, she may not be motivated to develop her skills because her talent allows her to be ahead of her competition without much effort. She therefore can coast into results compared to her peers.

It's important to note at this point that if you measure your success solely by comparison to your peers, you'll never win the world, because winning the world is contingent upon maximizing your own personal performance, regardless of how it compares to others. In other words, if you reach your maximum potential but still rank below others, you have still won the world as it pertains to you; you will have what you sought and the satisfaction that comes from it. But even if you rank number one, if you fall short of your own potential, you've failed to win the world, and you won't feel fulfilled. You'll always wonder what might have been.

Sometimes less talented people have a greater passion for certain activities than their more talented counterparts do. That passion can act as a supplement to talent. A child who enjoys the sport so much that his desire to play allows him to move past failure may have an advantage later in life. If he perseveres by practicing more than his talented counterparts, he may catch up to their natural talent with developed skill. If he does, he has a greater chance of long-term success than someone with more natural talent who did not practice as often.

His future success will be perpetuated by his treasure chest of experience and training habits. He will have formed habits that make him train harder, with longer duration and a higher level of sustained intensity than his peers.

It may sound counterintuitive, but research shows that experience gained from activities such as chess doesn't necessarily transfer to other board games. This is because chess is a particular kind of game with precise rules, and when a grandmaster plays other games, he only recalls past experiences from that particular game. But what does transfer for the grandmaster who acquired his success through hard work and experience is the past knowledge of what it takes to *train correctly*. Understanding how to develop a new talent is like learning a second foreign language. Knowing Spanish won't necessarily help you master a new challenge in life or work, but you come to know not only the language but the *process* of learning, so that when you face challenging times, you face them with optimism, because you know that you'll do what it takes to succeed. You then eliminate the mental errors that stem from emotional weaknesses. Ultimately, this streamlines training.

The old adage that "practice makes perfect" is true, but it's more involved than that. *Only perfect practice* makes practice perfect. And perfect practice requires intensity.

The most successful people in the world are intense. So, to put it bluntly, an intense person who goes through intense training has the greatest odds of success in life. In the next chapter, I'll address the essential building blocks of effective skill development, but we must first look at the current topic of intensity. Intensity makes strategy come to life. Intensity is the foundation. Without it, even the greatest training program will be weak.

One of the first shifts you should make is to stop thinking about "intense" people as hyper, loud, and obnoxious. This is an image of success portrayed by many radio personalities, TV stars, and sports figures, but it's not the whole picture. Intensity can be quiet as well. The great football star Walter Payton demonstrated that type of intensity. He was quiet on the sidelines, never taunted other players, and did not draw attention to himself with anything other than his results. But he was intense. He practiced harder than any other player on the team. He showed up earlier, stayed later, and ran harder. And during the off season, he punished himself with a famous routine of hill sprints.

I am convinced that almost any average, bench-warming high school running back could play at least Division III football if he committed himself to Payton's workout routine. Payton made a much better athlete of himself than most people do because of his training standards and intensity.

Most people are motivated to become good at something in life, whether it's golf, sales, card games, or parenting. The problem is that most people stop improving after reaching their current capacity instead of aiming long-term at their potential. As a result, they fall short. They reach a level of satisfaction, and then they relax their standards and intensity.

A man who takes up golf late in life may work hard to catch up to his friends' low scores. He might even startle his buddies as they watch him improve over his first few seasons. (They didn't see him sneaking in extra rounds each week and hitting buckets of balls after work every day.) He trained intensely to catch up. But what does he do once he does catch up? He backs off. He goes a few more years, and his score barely nudges down any further than it did the first couple of seasons. Frustration sets in, and he resigns himself to being "good enough." Later, he chalks his stagnant score up to the fact that golf is a difficult game and fails to realize that his improvement ended when his intense training was over.

Of course, at times it is prudent to back off. It doesn't make sense for a working husband and father to go from jogging a few miles a week, for the purpose of staying in shape, to running ultra marathons just to see how far he can go.

Likewise, it is justifiable for a late-in-life, weekend golfer to ease back on his golf time once he swings respectably with his peers. But it's not acceptable for a parent to stop child-rearing just because his child is not on drugs and dropping out of school. While this may sound like an exaggeration, it is unfortunately exactly the way some parents set standards. How many of us have heard parents say things such as, "Well, at least he's not on drugs," in order to justify other flaws in their child such as failing grades or disruptive behavior?

Allow me to develop this parenting example further because the relationship that a parent has with his or her child is in many ways the same type of relationship we are to have with ourselves. Parents are responsible for teaching children right from wrong by governing their actions. Parents set standards, make rules, and make sure their children abide by those rules. Of course, a parent must forgive a child when he makes a mistake, but she must also teach the child how to avoid the mistake in the future. This means disciplining the child. As an adult, you must also discipline yourself. Self-discipline is intense because it means restraining yourself from things you *want* to do in order to do things you *ought* to do.

That being said, parents who find themselves saying these things never *intended* to have their children fail in school. Usually, the parents start out with high hopes for their children. They read to them at night and teach them how to count, say the alphabet, and use their manners. These lessons are all quite intense. But somewhere along the line, they lower that intensity.

If a mother gets tired, she may begin to accept behaviors that she once found unacceptable. Beaten down by relentlessly being challenged, the mother watches her semi-well-behaved toddler become a not-so-well-behaved preschooler and eventually a pain-in-the-tail teenager. She resigns herself to the fact that her son is "strong-willed" and therefore not like those other nice kids who were just "born that way." "Besides," she says, "all teenagers are difficult."

Of course, that is all self-justification. The stronger willed the child is, the more the training needs to be intense. A strong-willed child is naturally intense, so if he is provided the service of intense training, he has great odds of winning the world. When things get tough, so should the training. That is true not only for children; it is true for adults as well.

The problem is that, as adults, we need to dole out the standards (which is easy), but then we need to live up to them (which is difficult). Every parent has an obligation to win the world when it comes to parenting skills. Learning how to raise an infant must be followed by learning how to raise a toddler, then a preschooler, all the way, stage-by-stage, through college.

Almost nobody denies this continuous responsibility for parents. Why then would it be acceptable to give up when your parents pass the baton to you? You are the one who takes over when your parents are through. It's your responsibility to continue the work your parents started, no matter how big the project is when you inherit it and no matter how old you are once you realize it.

It's easy for us to point the finger at other people who throw away their talent. It's easy to recognize the tragedy when a teenager throws away her future on drugs or other risky behaviors. Society cries out, "What a tragedy. She had such a bright future." This is simply a way of saying, "What a waste of potential."

Although it's easy to see wasted potential in other people, many of us fail to recognize our own wasted potential. A soul is a soul no matter who it belongs to, young or old, gifted or not, popular or obscure, someone else or ourselves. For anyone to neglect their own potential is a tragedy. So the intensity that a parent puts into the first years of child-rearing must be applied to the rest of the little one's childhood. Likewise, the intensity that we put into our own lives during our younger days of formal education, discovering the way the world works and developing relationships, must continue in some form as an adult.

The surprising thing is that this does not take as much effort as you might think. Dr. Donald Wetmore, a well-known time-management trainer, points out to his students that, if they took one hour a day for independent study, 365 days a year, then they could learn at the rate of a full-time student. Within three to five years, he says, they could become an expert in a topic of their choice. Three to five years goes fast. What do you want to be an expert in? What would you gain by stoking the fire of intensity and devoting yourself to a mission?

Winning Questions

1. Think of talents you had from an early age (physical, academic, etc.). What came naturally to you?

2. Did you shape your natural talents through training and practice, or did you let them "take care of themselves"?

3. Have you known anyone (including yourself) who was talented at something at an early age but did not

follow through in developing the talent? Why do you think there was no follow-through? (Boredom, other interests, etc.)

4. Have you ever had to work harder than others around you (in family, workplace, etc.) because they had more talent than you did for a particular task? What did you learn about your ability to learn and develop skill?

5. How can you apply this knowledge to your current life goals?

6. What are negative examples of "intense" people you have seen in your life and in the media? What qualities make such behavior negative? What about positive examples you have seen?

7. Have you known people who exhibited quiet intensity? What actions did they take that showed their intensity and dedication?

8. How can you model their behavior? Where do you lack intensity in your life?

9. Consider the golfer who was intense until he reached a certain goal. Have you had a similar experience in your own work and life? What led you to the intensity, and what led you to ease up on your intensity? Looking back over the experience, what might have happened if you'd continued your intensity?

10. Does it ever make sense to tone down your intensity? What goals should you always be intense about?

11. What is the first step you will take to increase your intensity where it matters?

Chapter Eight

FOUR KEYS FOR REACHING YOUR MAXIMUM SKILL LEVEL

INTENSITY IS a powerful strategy for training: the higher the intensity, the greater the skills. Intensity is not simply attitude or hype. It's a form of resolve. Intensity was in Mother Teresa and is in Donald Trump. No matter what skill you desire, it can be developed through intensity.

Intense training programs share the following four attributes:

1. Repetition

2. Frequency

3. Precision

4. Intention

Repetition

Repetition is an essential part of mastering any skill because it empowers you with experience beyond your years. Customers and clients almost always choose to hire professionals with lots of experience because experience increases the odds of good results. The way a professional *becomes* a professional is through repetition.

Consider the fact that true professionals practice their skills by repeating them to a mind-numbing degree. They make it look easy, but most of us never see the hard work behind it. We only see the glitz and glamour of the big game night, show debut, post-op discussion, or annual corporate address. Did you know that:

- A black belt in martial arts throws as many as 3 million kicks and 4 million punches before he earns that title.

- Tiger Woods makes a hundred short putts (four feet or less) in a row every night before he will end his daily practice. And if he misses even one putt, he starts over again.

- A virtuoso piano player has played the piano for thousands of hours before achieving that stature.

- The average committed mother may have to correct her child's behavior more than thirty thousand times before he is eighteen years old.

If you aren't on pace to reach your full potential, ask yourself why. Have you failed to put in the work to get the reward? How good could you be at something you love? Without repetition, you'll never know. One of the reasons people stop learning through repetition is because it *is* hard work. If I asked you to learn Swahili within the next six months, using a high-repetition immersion course, you'd probably have a hard time justifying the effort — the work would be very difficult. But if I told you I'd pay you five million dollars if you could speak Swahili within six months, I bet you'd be more interested in going through the effort. You'd probably commit every waking moment to learning, because the reward would be worth the work.

Of course, we don't all get paid five million dollars to develop random skills, but we do benefit in other ways. So act like there are five million reasons to develop them. The rewards will be there. Choose carefully where it makes sense for you to become an expert, and then pursue that mission with intensity.

Frequency

Frequency is the number of times something takes place within a certain period. For example, if you were to hear a new foreign alphabet twenty times in a row you might be able to memorize it. On the other hand, if you heard it just once a year, you probably wouldn't memorize it even over twenty years. Likewise, if you run two miles a hundred times in a year, you'd most likely lose weight and build endurance. But if you run two miles a hundred times over twenty years, you wouldn't build any endurance and probably wouldn't lose weight either. You would spend all your time relearning as though it were your first experience.

The more you pack together your repetitions, the faster and more permanently you'll learn new skills. Frequency is especially important in the early stages of learning. With it, a foundation is laid. Even though skills can erode over time, they are more likely to come back faster if the initial learning included a high frequency.

So if you're going to learn a new skill, be sure to schedule more time in the beginning to build a strong foundation. Then, after you are satisfied with your performance, you can ease back your training. (You should know, however, that there is a point where atrophy will set in if you ease back too far.)

Precision

As important as frequency and repetition are, a training program that utilizes them is incomplete without precision because what you *repeat,* you *learn.* If you practice with sloppiness, then you'll be sloppy. Experts become experts because they have high standards, not only for their workload but also for the accuracy of their work. A marksman who is developing his skills will not quit for the day just because he takes hundreds of shots at his target. He stops after he has hit the target hundreds of times. He is interested in precision. The accuracy with which he shoots is the measure of his success.

Many people confuse the feeling of hard work that accompanies frequency and repetition with results. But if you frequently and repetitively mispronounce a foreign language, you'll not only fail to communicate effectively, you'll need to undo the wrong learning if you want to correct the pronunciation.

Set the highest conceivable standard for yourself when you are developing your skills. Most people begin learning a skill with a romanticized image of how good they will be at it. Once they try the skill, they usually face challenges. When that happens, some just assume that they aren't made for that activity and lower their standards. True champions ramp up their resolve and push forward. Of course, not everyone is called to be good at everything, so sometimes it makes sense to back off, but in the important things in life, you must get past that temptation and aim high. You must know that developing skills is not easy. You will struggle, fail, and be challenged, but push yourself just an inch farther, a day longer, or a pound heavier, and you'll reach your goals. Expertise is for everyone.

If things get difficult early on, it's important to remember that the only thing you discover when you face a challenge early in your performance is your natural talent level. Talent is the starting point, but not the end. Your potential will not be reached as a result of the natural talent you have. It will be reached as a result of the training you put into developing your skills. So once you identify what you would like to pursue, practice with precision. There is no doubt that you'll need to work harder if you have less talent. But so what? Most people do.

If you expect to catch up to people who are more naturally talented, then your standards for training must be higher than theirs. That means you will need to put in more repetitions in a shorter period of time with a greater focus on precision than your more talented peers. Set accuracy goals if you want to learn faster. The goals themselves will help you stay focused. If the focus is on precision, you will require fewer repetitions to get an effective result. The combination of repetition, frequency, and precision in training is one that allows you to learn much more in a shorter period of time. This applies to intellectual skills as well as physical skills.

Intention

A trainer can demand extra repetitions, greater frequency, and more precision from you, but the biggest factor can't be drawn out by any trainer. This factor is your *intention* — the purpose you have behind developing the skills you desire. If you desire to develop your skills for entirely selfish purposes, then you must become entirely selfish in order to succeed. In today's culture, that is acceptable to many people. I remember an NFL coach who publicly admitted that he'd divorced his wife once he was hired as a head coach because he knew he needed to have a singular focus if he wanted to win the Super Bowl. His utilitarian approach to relationships was nauseating, though it did illustrate intention. Unfortunately, most people, like the NFL coach, who compromise relationships in order to get ahead end up regretting it. In the end, they may win the world, but they lose their souls.

Setting intentions for one area in life can lead to prosperity in other seemingly unrelated areas. In fact, I have met several leaders who have found ways to strengthen relationships when they intend to take their careers to the next level. A friend of mine found that owning his own business detracted from the time he could spend with his wife. Although she was very happy with her current work, they found a way for her to become part of his new business. She flourished in the environment, and their work interaction enhanced the rest of their time together. His intention was to build the business to great heights. He did that and increased his respect for his wife as he saw her prosper in her new role.

The desire to become good at something is strong because the rewards can be high. Recognition, money, power, and fame can all accompany a person with excellent skills. No doubt about it — these are enticing and highly motivational to a lot of people. The pot of gold at the end of the rainbow has motivated many people to develop their skills. But the intention of achieving one of these rewards works only in the short term. Over time, the purity of your intentions will be a major factor in your ability to continue a high level of training. If your intentions are to maximize your potential, then you're well on your way to longevity. If, on the other hand, your intentions are to bring glory to yourself, eventually you'll struggle and lose your soul.

One benefit of working for the purpose of reaching your potential is that the rewards I mentioned above — recognition, money, power, and fame — can accompany pure motives. If you stay grounded and remember your true intentions, these rewards will not distract you if they come your way. If they are your goal in the first place, however, then receiving them is like an end in itself. It can reduce your desire to continue tapping your potential.

Sometimes the pursuit of glory evolves into the desire to maximize your potential. After receiving money, fame, and power, people often feel empty. They wonder why they didn't get the satisfaction they longed for from their efforts. Some people react poorly to this emptiness and start acting out inappropriately. With proper reflection, however, they may shift their intentions and start to use their skills to do more. I went through this process myself. For years, I developed my business skills in order to climb the ladder. I certainly had the intention of providing for my family, and that did motivate me, but I never stopped to consider that God created me with a plan and that He gave me certain qualities to fulfill that plan.

Once I came to that realization, I took my skills to the next level. My motivation to become the best that I can possibly be began to grow and continues today. My intentions are not to reach a certain "thing" anymore. They are driven by a mission and a purpose. That does not mean that I don't have specific targets along the way. I still go to work to provide for my family and even to advance my career, but those intentions are not as final as they once were. I see beyond them.

When I prepared to break a stack of bricks for my second-degree Black Belt test in Tae Kwon Do, my instructor, Master Song, told me that when I hit the bricks, *something* will break. His ambiguity was intentional. He went on to explain that if I focused on the top brick, my wrist would break, but if I aimed through to the bottom brick, I would have the power to break through them all. Having a focus on a bigger goal than simply earning or advancing is like aiming at the bottom brick.

There's a lesson here for all of us. Think of the top brick as the most selfish aspect that exists in your life. It is what can "break" you if you focus only on it. The bricks beneath it relate to self-giving, such as to your organization, family, country, and God. Aiming at the lower bricks is what gives intention staying power and drives you through selfishness toward what is truly important.

The movie *Cinderella Man* portrays the true story of James J. Braddock, the depression-era fighter who came out of retirement after losing many fights. In the 1920s, he did well, but eventually he ran into a string of defeats. As the depression intensified, he suffered the same way many of his contemporaries did. He went from having a lot of money to having nothing. It was painful for him to watch his family suffer from cold and hunger, so when he was given a rare chance to make a comeback, he excelled beyond the expectations of all who knew him. He actually earned a shot at the title and won. Before the championship fight, he was interviewed at a press conference, and a reporter asked him what was responsible for his amazing turnaround. He told the reporter that, for the first time, he really knew what he was fighting for. "Well, what are you fighting for?" the reporter asked. Braddock simply replied, "Milk."

Even though you might only see the top brick right now, you are working for more. It's your obligation to see what bricks are beneath the surface and to aim at reaching them. You are born with your talent, but reaching your potential is achieved only through hard work. If you act with intention, then you'll work with intensity. No one can endure any activity that loses its purpose. Eventually, the fun fades or the pain of monotony grows too unbearable.

Winning Questions

1. Calling to mind our earlier discussion of unleashing your talent through skill and hard work, name two specific areas of your life where you could begin to use the power of frequency and repetition to maximize your potential.

2. In what training in your life could you take the next step in precision? What specific aspects would you have to change to achieve more precision in your training?

3. While thinking about the power of intention, answer James J. Braddock's question for your own life. What are *you* fighting for? What do you want more than anything for yourself and your loved ones?

❧ *Chapter Nine* ❧

DISCOVER THE POWER
OF BEING A FOLLOWER

W HEN MOST PEOPLE see the word "follower," they think of it as something negative. To be a successful person, don't you have to *stop* following and start leading? In fact, however, you can be a great person without being a great leader, and you'll never be a great leader unless you master being a follower. In America, there are thousands of books, seminars, and workshops being held in schools, offices, and conferences on the topic of leadership. Children are indoctrinated to "become leaders." With conviction, parents and teachers tell young people, "Don't be a follower!"

Advice like this has become part of our culture. But does it make any sense? If everyone leads, then who follows? It may shock you to learn that winning the world is not always about becoming a leader. Admittedly, when some people apply their gifts, they will inevitably become leaders, but winning the world is much more about knowing who to follow and how to follow them than it is about leading.

One day several years ago I sat in my boardroom awaiting a meeting with a group of people I didn't know. They had requested a meeting to discuss their plans to host a seminar. I was under the impression that they just wanted some input from me, since in the nature of my work I am involved in conducting and participating in seminars. They began the meeting by laying out a very comprehensive plan. When they completed their presentation, I remarked how well thought out the plan was and asked them why they felt the need to share all of this with me. They said, "We want you to be in charge of the project." "What do you mean?" I replied. "You have the plan laid out. You have the staff in place, and everything is in motion. I only have the knowledge of your program that you shared with me today. Why would you want me to take the leadership role? You all seem very capable."

Their answer was simple. "None of us want that type of role. We want *you* to tell *us* what to do by handing out the assignments." I told them that my schedule was full and that if I did decide to accept the offer, I would have very limited time. I explained that I literally would only have time to assign responsibilities, but no time to do any on my own.

They replied with the same conviction, telling me that they really *only* wanted me to tell them what to do, and that they would do all of the work. None of them was comfortable with the leadership role.

As surprised as I was when this happened, the conversation was a classic example of how each of us is different. Everyone in that room appeared to have the capacity to lead the task, but leading was not something that any of them enjoyed. They wanted to *follow,* but not because they lacked confidence, were afraid of responsibility, or felt inferior to a leader. They all handled their other jobs and responsibilities well and didn't run from hard work. In fact, the roles they wanted to keep for themselves involved *more* work than the one they asked me to take on. It just came down to their awareness of where they felt most comfortable.

My personality is quite the opposite, which is probably why they requested the meeting. I'm happy to follow the many great people I consider leaders in my life, but I'm much more comfortable in a leadership role. Leadership roles are invigorating for me because I enjoy the challenge. Of course, not everyone feels the same way. We are all different. Our gender, temperaments, upbringing, and education all help shape who we are and can affect our attitude about leading and following. And if you don't enjoy leading, that's genuinely okay. But whether or not you determine that leadership is your cup of tea, followership *has to* be.

No great leader would have ever been called great without great followers. Would Washington have crossed the Delaware had it not been for the brave and courageous men who followed him? Would John Hancock's signature be worth remembering if soldiers hadn't courageously fought for our independence? Would Vince Lombardi be a coaching icon without the Green Bay Packers?

The very old adage says that "behind every great man is a great woman." Similarly, behind every great leader (woman or man), there are great followers. Eisenhower served under General Patton, Michael Jordan followed Phil Jackson, and Mother Teresa followed Jesus. During their years of tutelage, they followed their leaders in obedience, albeit not always perfectly or enthusiastically.

But remember that Patton was once a follower too; so was Phil Jackson. At times great followers disagree with their leaders, but when push comes to shove, they store their differences of opinion into a bank of knowledge to be retrieved later. Then, when it comes time for them to lead, they can experiment with different philosophies. Sometimes, their ingenuity yields poor results, but often exerting their individuality in leadership is what makes them achieve even greater results.

So how can you become a better follower as you seek to win the world? Great followers share four common traits. They are:

- ◆ mission-oriented
- ◆ humble
- ◆ obedient
- ◆ prudent in choosing the right people to follow

Mission-Oriented

Effective followers always see the cause they are associated with as something bigger than themselves. This is easy to understand when it comes to causes such as freedom, health issues, or missionary work. But how can an employee at a local hot dog stand see the mission of selling hot dogs as something bigger than he is? Great followers don't see missions as *more valuable* than their dignity or personhood. Instead, they see missions as worth the commitment.

A soldier who is willing to die for his country considers freedom a worthy cause, but he does not believe that his life is less valuable than the mission. Instead, he sees it as a possible contribution to the mission. He invests himself into the cause, and that is what makes him effective. He will be valuable to the degree that he does invest himself.

A hot dog stand employee who would be willing to offer his life for the cause of serving hot dogs might be teetering on insanity. If an armed robber came by with the purpose of stealing the hot dog cart, it would be rational and prudent for the employee to let him take the money or the stand. But that's appropriate because the mission of a hot dog vendor is not to save lives or to preserve freedom. It is probably more like, "To serve a great-tasting hot dog at a reasonable price in a convenient manner."

In practical terms, making the mission bigger than you means that if you run out of ketchup but don't "feel like" running to the store for more, you do it anyway. The cause is bigger than your fatigue. It also means that if you are crabby when you arrive at work, you put away your bad attitude and serve the hot dogs with a smile.

Parents can help instill this perspective into their children by setting high standards, particularly during their younger days when conditions are unfavorable. For example, if a child is unruly because it's past his bedtime, some parents excuse the behavior, but that only teaches the child that being tired is a legitimate reason to misbehave. Effective parents gently but firmly enforce the same standards for their children, whether they are tired or not.

It's easy to be kind and even tempered when things are going well, but champions are made during difficult times. Remaining committed to a mission is also easy when you're *succeeding* in the mission, but it is when times get tough that enduring commitment matters. Training a child to control his temper when he is tired is difficult but always worth it. That training prepares the child for the real world. It prepares him to commit to certain missions even when his feelings are not in line with the cause. It also teaches him self-control, the ability to put his intellect ahead of his feelings. So if he becomes a hot dog vendor and he feels like verbally lashing out at an unreasonable customer even when he knows intellectually it's the wrong thing to do, he will bite his tongue and do what is right. Adults are tired and angry quite often in life, but they must control their attitudes and behaviors in the midst of trials.

To win the world, you must have self-control. If you didn't learn this essential skill from your parents, you must commit to learning it now. If you see your followership roles as stepping-stones to becoming a leader, then you must especially learn self-control. The way you handle yourself as a leader often defines business culture. Leaders without self-control lead people into chaos. But leaders who can put the company's mission first will always see their actions and reactions in light of the larger goal. This mission-oriented approach can be difficult, and self-control will be needed whenever you'd rather satisfy your short-term feelings than the long-term mission. But losing yourself in any good mission can make life a bit more enjoyable. And at the end of the day, you may not only serve a hot dog; you might make someone smile. And that is a worthy cause.

Humble

A follower with pride is a follower who will fail. Pride blinds everyone, followers included. Any leader will tell you that *humble* followers are the most reliable, competent, level-headed, and effective people in their organizations. Humility is not wimpiness; it is precision truth. Humble people don't overestimate their skills — or underestimate them. They have an accurate assessment of themselves, and as a result they have the ability to more accurately see their role in any given cause or assignment.

When a humble person is asked to carry out assignments, she will see past subjective disagreements she may have about strategies and approaches. She will acquiesce to requests without huffing and puffing and will work hard to reach the goals set forth by her leaders. At the same time, her humility will give her the strength to respectfully suggest other potential options when she is certain that those suggestions would be beneficial.

Humble people can gain unique insights into other people's actions and words because humble people have clean consciences and carry very little baggage. Emotional baggage is usually the major source of confusion for prideful people. It confuses their ability to take direction and to carry out tasks.

Pride also prevents followers from being able to discern whether or not their leaders are taking them to a healthy destination. Humility acts as a filter to see things as they currently exist without the distortion many of us see because of our own personal histories. Like humble leaders, humble followers observe keenly, speak only the necessary number of words, and do not bad-mouth other teammates.

Just to repeat: humility is not the same as being mumbly-mouthed and beating up on yourself. If you can learn to honestly assess your strengths and weaknesses and be attentive to how you can contribute to your current goals, you will be able to cultivate the humility needed for all followers.

Obedient

The term "obedience" is definitely no longer in style! It is a word that conjures up oppression more than acquiescence and tyranny rather than loyalty, but the classic synonyms for "obedient" are: well-trained, dutiful, respectful, and compliant. People don't want to be obedient in today's world because they feel that obedience is equal to blind following and weakness. "I don't want to be obedient! I'm not a dog!" This fear of weakness might be accurate if you choose to follow the wrong leaders, but obedience to the right leaders is actually a form of personal empowerment.

A batting coach, for example, gives a baseball player three suggestions for improving his swing. The player can ignore the coach and do it his own way, or he can be obedient to his coach. Most likely, if he listens, he'll improve his batting average. The result is not oppressive; it's liberating. The obedient player can master his skills at an accelerated pace because he's tapping into wisdom and experience he hasn't lived long enough to possess on his own. In this sense, obedience is like good science. Scientists don't spend all of their time reinventing the wheel. Some ideas are well-tested laws; others are useful and provisional guesses. A great science professor can help a budding scientist learn to identify what is the certain and sure information about his field. Obedience, then, doesn't mean failing to think for yourself — it means accepting wisdom, direction, and coaching for the purpose of accomplishing a mission.

Obedience accelerates learning because it opens your mind to the teachings of others. Socrates' teachings influenced Plato, who in turn taught Aristotle. Each of these great thinkers had some fundamentally similar ideas and, at the same time, very different conclusions. Aristotle was not *oppressed* by his training under Plato, and the many students who flocked to the ancient Academy weren't limited or enslaved by the teaching they received there, as strict as it was. By training their minds under a great master who had more experience than they did, they were able to learn to think for themselves.

It's invaluable to have a strong foundation to work from, and great followers recognize that good leaders can provide that foundation. They spend little time debating the fundamentals that their mentors teach them until they master them for themselves. If you have experience leading people, you know this already. If you've ever led people who constantly question or interrupt your "teachings," you've probably answered something like, "Just do it, and you'll see." If you're currently striving to be a follower, bear that in mind as well whenever you're tempted to spend more time asking questions than practicing the advice. The energy it takes to debate with a leader on menial topics can be taxing and unbeneficial to all parties. If you're obedient to the right people, you'll use their strengths until you can own them for yourself.

Choosing the Right People to Follow

Choosing the right people to follow can make all the difference. If Plato had lived in a different era, say, the nineteenth century, would he have been influenced by the philosophies of Marx instead of Socrates? How might he have developed his own philosophy if he had been given a different foundation? Would he have recognized Marx's false theories about human nature? It's hard to say; even very smart people can be misled. But picking the right leader makes all the difference, so it's important to spend time thinking about who you follow, and why.

Not all people or ideas deserve to be followed. A baseball player could choose a coach who doesn't know what he's doing, and a scientist may subscribe to scientific "facts" that are either impossible to prove or demonstrably untrue. Young businesspeople sometimes unknowingly choose to work for incompetent leaders with poor business philosophies. Such an error may retard their careers. On the other hand, others choose exceptional leaders who help thrust them far ahead of the pack. Spending time choosing who to follow is much more important than spending time questioning leadership. If you were a basketball player and you wanted to be on a winning team, it would make sense to seek out a coach with a winning record. Once you find him, it would make no sense to question everything he tells you. Just follow his lead and assimilate into his greatness. Become a part of his future success in order to build upon your own.

In my opinion, leaders rank high on the "choose carefully" list — just below spouse! Here are five quick questions to ask yourself before following someone so that when you decide to follow, you can do it with confidence:

1. What is the leader's track record for success?
2. How did the leader get to where he or she is? Was he appointed? Did she merit it? (Follow merit if possible, and be cautious of appointed leaders.)
3. Does the leader buy into the mission he is supposed to be leading people in?
4. Does the leader paint a clear picture of where she is taking you?
5. Does the leader's past demonstrate trustworthiness?

Jean François Gravelet, a tightrope walker who was better known as Blondin, became famous for tightrope walking across Niagara Falls in 1859. He repeated the stunt several times, making it more and more thrilling by varying his approach. He did it blindfolded, while pushing a wheelbarrow, on stilts, and ultimately while carrying his promotional manager, Harry Colcord, on his back.

During the crossing, Harry, who was afraid of heights, stared in fear at the waters 190 feet below. Then he looked at the 1100 feet that they needed to cover and began swaying to keep steady. Blondin gave him the most motivational "followership" message I have ever heard:

"Harry, you are no longer Colcord; you are Blondin. Until I clear this place, be part of me — mind, body, and soul. If I sway, sway with me. Do not attempt to do any balancing yourself. If you do, we shall both go down to our death."

Harry thankfully picked the right leader, and they survived. When you find the right person to follow, trusting that person is the best strategy, and it can lead to prosperity. If you pick the wrong leader, then problems are inevitable.

In a formal, structural sense, followership is for everybody, but leadership is only for those called to lead. Ironically, by their ability to learn the right kinds of information and learn it rapidly and attentively, great followers are often elevated to the formal position of leader, and even if they are not, they will be perceived as leaders by way of their example. Being a great follower opens up many doors of opportunity in life and provides you with choices that can be fulfilling. A great follower who is offered a leadership role may be gratified by taking on the new role and may thrive in the environment. Likewise, a great follower who turns down a leadership role because he knows himself well can also feel satisfied. He will know that his work is valued, and he'll inevitably lead by example, even if he does not formally carry the responsibility.

Winning Questions

1. What are some negative ideas that come to mind when you think of "following"?

2. Have you ever had leaders who you now think were not the right people to follow? In what settings did you work with them (business, home life, neighborhood, politics...)? Why did they turn out not to be the right leaders to follow?

3. How do you see the difference between leaders who are worth following and those who should not be followed?

4. Identify one person in your current situation who you think you could learn from by becoming more of a follower. If there is no one, think of one way you could make changes to your life to have contact with a leader who is worth following.

5. Someday, challenge yourself to become a mentor to someone else.

❧ *Chapter Ten* ❧

TRUE FREEDOM: BEING GRATEFUL FOR WHO YOU ARE AND WHAT YOU HAVE

THE WORD "win" presupposes competition. You can win the lottery, chess, baseball games, and wars — and in each case, someone loses. Some victories are based on luck, others on skill, hard work, and guts. The most important victories are a combination of all three.

Charlie Rose once asked Warren Buffet why Buffet was so successful. To paraphrase, Mr. Buffet said he was lucky. *Lucky,* he said, because he was born in a free country. He acknowledged that there was effort involved. He admitted that he applied himself, but he emphasized luck. He explained that he was lucky because, for reasons outside of their control, so many of the six billion people living today never had the opportunity to develop their talent. His gratitude for being born in a free country was evident, and that gratitude motivated him to apply himself.

Gratitude is an important first step in winning the world. If you are filled with gratitude, you'll have a stable foundation. For example, we honor and even romanticize the "greatest generation" because of the spirit in which they fought for freedom in World War II. They fought with gratitude. Of course, some fought reluctantly, but most of the romance is true. Gratitude wins wars. It is more powerful than hate and greed, and it lasts longer than the hunger for power. And in their gratitude for their freedom, that generation emulated the gratitude they saw in their parents, many of whom were immigrants who understood from bitter experience how unique America was as the land of freedom.

Today, it is common to criticize young people for their lack of gratitude, especially when it comes to freedom. Many claim that young people today don't even know the origins of their freedom. That is an unfair blanket statement because, as I write this, thousands of young men and women are defending our liberties throughout the world. They serve with gratitude the same way the greatest generation did. There is, however, some truth to the sentiment. Many young people today just don't realize how difficult it is to secure freedom, and this ignorance renders them ungrateful.

People who are ungrateful don't fight for noble causes and rarely lead productive lives. Instead, they complain and pout while everyone else around them goes to work. It is nearly impossible to win anything, let alone the world, if you don't value the prize.

What's more, people without gratitude don't simply lack gratitude; they usually develop un-gratitude and become dark and negative about life. This pessimistic sentiment is mocked in the tacky yet Tony Award–winning Broadway play *Avenue Q*. The opening song, "It Sucks to

Be Me," is meant as a kind of exaggeration, but it really gets to the heart of what many people today believe about their lives — that they have a miserable existence.

This is unfortunate because in reality, it's great to be you. You have a unique set of experiences that have formed who you are today. Some of them came in the outward appearance of defeat, while others arrived as obvious successes. Both outcomes can be used for good in the future. You have unique insights and knowledge — or at least potential for knowledge. You have distinctive interests and special tastes that form who you are and what you are best suited to do. You won the lottery of customization. And for those reading this book in a free country, you are envied by billions. But none of that will come to life if you aren't grateful for what you have and who you are.

Freedom is, of course, not free. It is won through blood, sweat, tears, and even death. To maintain freedom, it is sometimes necessary to continue to fight. This is true when it comes to national security, and it's also true for individuals. I am talking about personal freedom. It's tragic to watch an innocently imprisoned person struggle in captivity. But even more tragic is to witness a free person voluntarily living in his own bondage, enslaved to his own ingratitude, apathy, and self-imposed limitations.

If you have not yet considered how great you can be, it's time. It's time to maximize your potential by winning the world without losing your soul. In order do this, you must win the war that is closest to home: the war between you and yourself. It is a war for peace made possible only through hard work. You must die to your old self and live as a new person empowered by gratitude and resolve. You must continue to fight the inner battle of self-doubt, ingratitude, and apathy that threatens your freedom. These inner opponents of freedom are not always as obvious as enemies of the state. More commonly, your adversaries in this war are subtle things like vices, addictions, self-doubt, and despair.

Although these inner enemies are different in nature than the enemies of a country, you must fight them in a similar way. You must set up a "personal defense" department that emulates a national defense department. Your goal should be to prevent war, but if war becomes inevitable, you must ensure victory. You must use mental diplomacy, fight to win with resolve, and begin with the end in mind.

All of these actions are carried out ultimately to find peace. If peace were guaranteed among nations, the trillions of dollars spent throughout the world on security would be a waste of money, but peace is not guaranteed. A ready defense is prudent, and it takes energy and commitment to make it effective. Part of that commitment is developing your talent and skill in the same way that national defense trains Special Forces. That will be the focus of the next several chapters.

Winning Questions

1. What are three gifts and freedoms you enjoy today that many others in the world do not enjoy?

2. What parts of your life inspire your gratitude? In what areas of life do you have gifts to be thankful for, even though you don't feel gratitude?

3. Take ten minutes now to think about one aspect of your life where you want to practice gratitude for what you've been given. Think about how you came to have that gift (through good luck, hard work, etc.). Then think about all that was required for that gift to come to you (good health, the hard work of others, etc.). Try for these ten minutes to become more aware of how good that gift is.

4. Based on this new awareness, what will you do to nurture your gratitude? How will it guide your actions as you seek to win the world without losing your soul?

❧ *Chapter Eleven* ❧

IS LOSING YOUR SOUL A RELATIVE MATTER?

I F YOU WANT to win the world, you must be grounded in reality. You must objectively assess your talents, opportunities, and situations. It's impossible to be grounded if you subscribe to fashionable sentiments like, "That may be your truth, but it's not mine." Most people who say this do so in the name of tolerance. Tolerance is a valuable quality, but sacrificing objectivity in order to be tolerant is a mistake. When it comes to genuine truths and not just opinions, it isn't possible for people to have two opposing truths. If "my" truth is that $2 + 2 = 5$ and your truth is that $2 + 2 = 4$, I'm simply wrong and need to correct my viewpoint. To claim that we are both entitled to our own "truths" on the matter is unreasonable.

No doubt, we are entitled to our own opinions and beliefs; but the act of believing something does not make it true. No one owns truth; it stands outside of all people. I don't own the truth about gravity, and neither do you. Even if I didn't believe in gravity, I would still be subject to its laws, regardless of the sincerity of my disbelief.

What I have described above is "relativism," which, for the sake of this book, is a term I use to refer to the belief that there is no such thing as absolute truth. It claims, for example, that morals and morality are dictated by cultures, which can change. Relativists declare that one can never really know anything...and *that's a fact.* Of course, as many have pointed out, relativism of this kind collapses in on itself. If nothing at all is certain, then a relativist has no basis for saying with such certainty that "nothing is certain."

In an effort to avoid being judgmental, to avoid confrontation, or even to justify dubious personal behaviors, everyone is capable of slipping into relativistic thinking. Claiming that everyone can be right or that your actions are always justified because of the situation leads to what ethicists call ethical or moral relativism.

If you think about it for a moment, you can probably recall several people you know who are guilty of this. It's easy to point fingers at the relativists you know, but be warned: we *all* sometimes fall into that trap. As you read the examples in this chapter, reflect on how some of these situations might apply to you as well.

Being in tune with reality means accepting what is true even when it's difficult to take. Relativists never win the world because they lack the objectivity it takes to identify personal strengths and weaknesses that allow for reaching maximum potential. Even if they find success in one aspect of their lives, they are miserable in others. Relativists often give in to personal temptations by justifying mistakes and taking shortcuts. They ignore weaknesses by removing objective standards, which is not acceptable if you want to win the world. As you develop your skills, grow in maturity, and gain experience, you'll inevitably have more responsibility. More responsibility can mean more stress, and this can easily lead to the temptation to cut corners in order to manage that stress.

Seeking only to win the world without concern for losing your soul always ends in disaster. You may remember the power of the 1970/80s-era Broncos/Raiders defensive end Lyle Alzado. He was one of the meanest, strongest men in the NFL. There were few people on the field more intimidating. I marveled at what I thought was his natural strength, but, like many others, I marveled in ignorance. Shortly after he retired, he shrank down to a fraction of his playing size because he stopped taking steroids. His size and strength had been artificially manufactured by anabolic steroids. His legacy drifted into a faint memory because people perceived that he did not earn his success but stole it. A few short years later, he became seriously ill and traced his sickness back to his steroid use. During the last years of his life, he spoke out publicly against the use of steroids in an effort to make up for his mistake by helping others avoid taking the path he took.

Alzado was filled with regret and wished he had never taken steroids. Most people who watched him during his prime thought he had won the world. He was a two-time All-Pro, he racked up 97 sacks in 196 games, and he was a nearly household name in the United States. But behind the scenes he was miserable.

He once estimated that he spent as much as $30,000 a year on the steroids, often buying them at various gyms throughout the country. His second wife stated that mood swings caused by steroids ended their marriage. Although he was never arrested for physically abusing her, she called the police at least five times for that reason when they were together.

It's easy to envy people we see on TV or the Internet, but if we strive to become like them, we want to be sure to imitate what they do best and consider the price they have paid for their success. Whenever you find success the easy way, you only fool yourself. Everyone eventually pays the price for cheating.

Think of what happens as we grow up. In early childhood we all test the waters of rebellion. Even though preschoolers are not morally or ethically culpable for their actions, they must be trained to exercise self-control and good judgment so that when they reach the age of reason, they will be capable of making sound decisions.

As they advance in age, they grow in culpability until they are no longer excused for their actions. If they are not held accountable by their parents, their teachers will attempt to provide that training. If they fail, then a sheriff or warden might be the only person to offer that service. Then they become a menace to society.

The rebellious things that little ones do will grow into bigger issues if they are not corrected, and they can be corrected only if common rules are put in place. In other words, if parents raise their children by teaching them that it is morally permissible to cheat, then they will have to be corrected in school on the basis of the school's understanding of right and wrong. You can imagine the confusion for that child. A universal common thread of honesty is the only thing that keeps order, which makes it a definitive rule to live by. That common thread is found in the natural law that universally underpins moral issues. For example, since the beginning of time it has been wrong to abuse children. Such a heinous thing is still wrong today and always will be wrong in the future. That fact transcends culture and hits intrinsically at the core of who we are as human beings.

When you teach children absolutes such as "don't lie," "don't cheat," and "don't steal," they learn and you have order. When you make moral issues a matter of personal choice, you have chaos. The result is that relativism is the greatest cause of division in the world. When everyone lives by different standards of morals, ethics, justice, and retribution, disharmony results. There is a saying that if you always tell the truth, you never need to remember what you said. This saying points to a deeper truth, which is that the truth is liberating and makes life simpler. You need that simplicity if you want to go big by winning the world. This simple, universal understanding of honesty is the only definition that translates from person to person, culture to culture, without complication. Of course, there *are* complicated moral issues in life that need careful examination, but if the basic starting place for honesty is not rock-solid, then there is no chance at unity or good decision making.

In the name of tolerance, some students in public schools are sheltered from moral training. For the most part, public schools condemn the explicit teaching of morality because, oddly enough, it would be "immoral" to push any specific morality on the students. This decision has led to increased cheating, violence, sexual activity, and lower test scores. So in an effort to gain order, they sometimes substitute morality with "ethics," which is a trend that continues in colleges and corporations across America. Ethics is defined as "the study of morality's effects on conduct and a code of morality."

Substituting the word "ethics" is simply putting a veneer on the issue. If "ethics" is an acceptable topic for the boardroom and the classroom, then what is the moral code that ethics is based on? Ethics could be any of the following:

- What your parents taught you

- What your church or religion teaches you (this varies tremendously depending on the religion, even inside different forms of, say, Christianity, Islam, Hinduism, Judaism, and Buddhism)

- What the law of the land mandates

- What you feel personally obliged to do

- What famous people tell you is moral

- What you can get away with

So who has the right moral code? One way to find true moral teachings is to use reason, which is never in conflict with the natural law. It is common sense that tells us that honesty taught at home = honesty reinforced at school = honesty in the workplace = a healthy society = a healthy next generation. If honesty taught at home is different from honesty taught at school, which is different from honesty taught in the workplace, then there is really no such thing as honesty. If you offer every separate individual, household, school, and workplace a different definition of honesty, you have division and chaos.

So the only moral code that is consistent for all people is the one found in the natural law, because it supersedes religious customs, cultures, and government laws. A great way to assess what is consistent with natural law is to put issues to the test of time. When it comes to morality, just like science, what has always been true always will be true. For example, no one at any time in history has ever felt it was just for items that are rightfully his to be stolen from him, and no one ever will. No one in history thought it was just to be assaulted for no reason, and no one ever will.

Embedded in those examples is another test to determine consistency with the natural law. It is the golden rule. Ask yourself if the things you do to others would be moral if they were done to you. This may seem like an obvious guideline, but it's not so obvious in the messiness of day-to-day living. Some people, for example, have no trouble lying to others, but when someone lies to them, they cry "foul."

Natural law is evident in our lives, but it takes humility to accept it. If you begin your search for the truth about any issue by saying, "How can I prove that I'm right?" or "How can I prove that she is wrong?" without considering what is actually true, you'll never recognize the truth when you find it.

If you want to remain objective, you must have humility. This means knowing in advance that you won't always be right and that you're bound to make mistakes. Owning up to them is paramount to winning the world. Pride is what fuels relativists. The last thing they want is someone telling them what they can or can't do even though they have no problem telling others what to do.

In the following chapter you'll learn how to weave your way around a relative world in an objective way. Working effectively with relativists requires knowing what their rules for morality are. It also necessitates knowing what might change those rules. Once you have that information, you must become attuned to the thinking of relativists as often as possible, because their morality is determined by feelings and by the ebb and flow of culture, which can change quickly.

Winning Questions

1. Review the list of moral codes on page 114. Where do you draw your own ethical standards when it comes to relationships? The workplace? Family life?

2. Regardless of which ones influence you the most, which of these sources seem to change the most? Which ones seem the most constant and reliable?

ACHIEVING ABSOLUTE SUCCESS IN A RELATIVE WORLD

BEING COMMITTED to winning the world without losing your soul means knowing how to navigate your way around immorality. This will make you unpopular at times. It may not be inspiring to know this, but odds are that at some point in your life, you will work in an environment with a corrupt culture, corrupt people, and corrupt business practices. But no matter how bad it is, you can't succumb to the "everyone else is doing it" mentality.

As this book has made clear, the most crucial thing for followers to do is to pick the right leaders. Likewise, because the world is filled with corruption, it's important to choose your friends and business partners wisely whenever possible. One key here is to realize that it's not always your choice to make. Obviously, you can't choose your brother-in-law, and you don't have any control over who buys the house next door. Likewise, at work, you may not do the hiring, which means you don't have any control over who your co-workers are.

It's pretty easy to identify people who are corrupt to the core because they unashamedly disregard any moral code. Their blatancy makes them fairly easy to size up and avoid, whereas relativists are harder to identify. Relativists normally don't title themselves as such, and many would actually deny that they are relativistic. But they can still be recognized by certain beliefs. The most common cliché that describes relativists is: "Everyone has a price." This means that no matter how moral a person claims to be, if the price is right he will compromise his principles. I don't believe that jaded opinion to be totally true: there are incredibly virtuous people in the world. But the saying is a good one for each of us to consider, not to point the finger at others but to remain honest ourselves. When do others say such things? And when do we find ourselves saying what amounts to the same thing?

The following story best illustrates a typical relationship life cycle with a relativist:

A young Native American boy was sent by his tribe to fetch water. He searched but came up empty. Then he heard a voice ask, "What are you looking for?" Much to his surprise, it was a snake asking the question. "Water," the boy replied. The snake answered, "I know where water is. It is at the top of the mountain. I am thirsty too. Carry me to the top of the mountain, and I will show you where the water is." Then the boy quivered, "But you are a snake; you'll bite me." The snake seduced back with, "No, I won't; you can see that I am friendly. It will be fun. Take me with you." Convinced by the snake's smile and charm, the boy picked him up and they made their way to the top, laughing and singing the entire way. Just before the boy put the snake back on the ground, he screamed in pain and shock. "You said you wouldn't bite me!" cried the boy. "I know, but it's in my nature...," the snake hissed as he slithered away.

An unpleasant experience for the boy, but we can learn something from it. Relativists are usually nice people (remember: unfortunately, we all can be relativists at times), people you can trust—but only when the conditions are right. When people don't believe in absolute truth, very little prevents them from lying to you, stealing from you, or gossiping about you. All it takes for them to justify their actions is changing their belief to fit the situation. Instead of conforming their thinking and behavior according to what is true, they twist the "truth" to fit their feelings about the situation.

Ironically, most relativists claim to be moral, but because they believe that morality can change, they always have a moral loophole no matter what they do. That means a relativist who likes you is likely to be honest with you *because* he likes you. His moral code may state that "it's immoral to steal from people you like." Similarly, a relativist who gets paid well might believe that "it's immoral to lie to people who pay you well." But if these people stop liking you or feel that they are not getting paid enough, then watch out. In the mind of a relativist, it may be justified to cheat on the expense reports *because* he is not paid enough. Likewise, a relativist might lie to you *because* he stopped liking you.

Most relativists would not be brazen enough to walk into a store to steal something. But what might happen if a relativist picked up a pack of gum as she entered a store, got into a long conversation with a friend, and then accidentally walked out while forgetting to pay? If her moral code says that it's wrong to steal, she might go back in to pay. But what if her moral code has little qualifiers such as the following?

It is wrong to steal gum at the grocery store unless...

- it is from a really big store that would never miss the 50 cents anyway.

- you know you can get away with it.

- it is an accident like this was. Besides, in the past, I've spent so much money there that they practically owe me.

- I'm already in my car. If I'd noticed earlier, I'd pay for it.

- there are other extenuating circumstances. (I ripped my jacket on a hanger in their store while I was there, so this is justice anyway.)

Compare those justifications with the response of a moral absolutist:

It is wrong to steal gum at the grocery store unless...

- Nothing. It's just wrong.

Who do you want shopping for gum *in your store?* Of course, just because a moral absolutist believes that stealing the gum is wrong doesn't guarantee that he would honor his belief, but the likelihood for him to go back in to pay is much higher. If he does fall short of his professed standards, at least he can measure them for the future.

The problem of relativism is not a merely abstract one. Research done in 2002 by Dr. Don McCabe shows a virtual moral collapse among students. His survey of forty-five hundred high school students determined that 75 percent of them have cheated at least once on a test. This is up from 50 percent in 1993 and a far cry from the 25 percent reported in 1963. The most startling of all the statistics is that 50 percent of the students who cheated (that's over a third of *all students*) did not think that copying questions and answers from a test was considered cheating. In an additional survey done by ABC Primetime Polls, 34 percent of students said they would be more likely to cheat if they knew they would not get caught.

Would you be more likely to cheat...

	Yes	No
if you knew you'd never be caught?	34%	65%
if you had a teacher who didn't seem to care about you and your work?	28	71
if it was in a class that didn't matter?	16	83
if you knew other students were cheating and by being honest you might get a lower grade?*	14	85

---

*Source: *abcnews.com*. ABCNEWS Primetime poll, by ICR-International Communications Research of Media, Pa.

Many students admit that lots of cheating happens simply because it's easy to do. There are websites to teach students how to cheat. One such website provides various ways to appear to be a good student while actually being a fraud. The people who run the website justify their "service" as something needed because of the unfair standards put on students and the "boring" material. The condescending tone of their message is a blatant manifestation of relativism. Hundreds of websites offer completed term papers as a free downloadable service. It's pretty easy to see the effect of this thinking as these people graduate and enter the work force.

Since relativists believe that morality can change based on culture, it's important for you to understand how they determine morality. This knowledge will be useful for you when you interact with people who think with a relativist perspective. It will also aid in keeping you from falling into the same thinking. If you want to win the world, you need to be able to identify these errors held by popular culture:

1. If most people do it, then it is moral.

2. If it's legal, it is moral, and if it's illegal, it is immoral.

3. If no one gets hurt, then it is moral.

4. If everyone agrees to it, then it is moral.

If most people do it, then it is moral.

If by next week, the majority of people voted to "euthanize" anyone who couldn't hold down a job, would that make it moral? Right now, society tells us that murdering the unemployable is immoral. But if attitudes changed, would the attitudes alone be enough to change the morality of such an act? Of course not. There is obviously something bigger than society that underpins this understanding.

You may think that is an extreme example. But consider that Hitler sent tens of thousands of mentally disabled and psychologically challenged German citizens to the gas chambers *before* the war because he considered them unproductive. He began by slowly lowering the inhibitions of doctors and soldiers by introducing the concept under the guise of "mercy killing." He strategically and deliberately conditioned them to think in relativistic terms: human life is not valuable in and of itself; there are exceptions. As a result, he established a regime of killers who eventually thought nothing of killing millions of people simply because of their Jewish heritage.

It's easy to illustrate this point by using extreme examples, but in real-life situations it can be more difficult to sift through. Cheating on taxes and spreading rumors are often justified by personal circumstances. Even some people who claim to live by a stronger moral code may cheat on taxes, justifying their actions on the basis of factors like having a large family to support. In other words, they claim that if they did not have this burden, they would pay. Some might add to the justification by rationalizing that most people cheat anyway, so it's really not so bad.

You can't win the world by following the crowd. When you get tempted to cut corners just because everyone else is doing it, stop and think for yourself. Does the action you're tempted to take go against your dignity? Does it make your conscience twinge? If so, take the narrow road by following your conscience, educating yourself, and doing what is right, not what is popular.

The sliding scale of morality does not change the essence of the act. Gossiping because you don't like someone is no better than gossiping about someone you do like. To win the world, consider the essence of the act, not your personal situation or how many people do the same thing.

If it's legal, it is moral, and if it's illegal, it is immoral.

Every day thousands of court cases are heard. In theory, each of them is heard in order to bring justice. Congress is supposed to introduce bills in order to protect citizens and the well-being of our nation. According to certain laws it is illegal to lie, cheat, steal, assault, and kill. The laws, which determine the legal status of these actions, were passed for the purpose of maintaining peace and order. But even though they have a moral tone to them, not all laws reflect morality.

It used be illegal to commit adultery. This was considered a breach of the wedding agreement. But as society's attitude about sexuality changed, the legal status of adultery also changed. It went from being a crime to a matter of personal choice. It is the right of men and women to discard their vows or to "upgrade" to a better spouse for any reason.

Does the societal shift toward accepting sexual liberties and personal choice make adultery moral or divorce no big deal? Today in many jurisdictions it's easier to get out of marriage than out of a lease. If the law accepted no-fault divorce reasoning to determine the binding of lease agreements, then no one would rent property. "Judge, I want out of my lease because I want out of my lease; things didn't work out the way I planned."

What if it became legal to physically overtake any home you wanted in America? Would that make it moral? That may seem farfetched, but America has a history of laws that were passed because of their moral nature, which have been reversed. No matter where you stand on these emotionally stirring issues today, you should reflect on the fact that most people used to believe that preemptive attacks on foreign countries, abortion, unwilling seizure of a home for the building of a private venture, sodomy, and no-fault divorce would never be legal *because they simply were immoral.* Even less emotionally stirring laws that have changed, such as spitting on sidewalks and using profane language in public, were on the books because the acts were considered immoral. Don't get sidetracked by your own assessment of whether these changes are good or bad. Just ask yourself: is it possible that these things could have all become moral *simply because the laws changed?* Were they immoral when they were illegal? The point is not to argue for or against each issue here. It is simply to make the case that the law does not determine morality. Deep down, everyone realizes that morality is deeper than something as malleable as certain laws.

This point is especially interesting because of an obvious contradiction. Most relativists claim that if the culture accepts something to be moral, then it is moral. At the same time, many of the same relativists claim that the law determines morality. But that does not pass the logic test. Abortion was made legal through the courts at the same time polls still showed that most people believed it was immoral. So is morality based on the law or the polls? Because these are irreconcilable, the default moral indicator for relativists is personal opinion. But if personal opinion determines morality, then anyone could kill anyone just because that person *personally believed* it was moral. That obviously does not work either.

Another example is prohibition. Was drinking alcohol intrinsically immoral because it was outlawed? If so, did legalizing alcohol again make it moral? There is no doubt that many laws are made to ensure moral conduct in America, but the whimsical changing of laws of the land can't manipulate the natural law.

Geographical and physical locations are another intriguing wrinkle in the philosophy that the law establishes morality. It is illegal to steal in America but, hypothetically speaking, if it were legal to steal in Canada, would that mean it's immoral to steal in America and moral to steal in Canada? Physical location cannot change the nature of stealing. So as you can see, the idea that the law determines morality collapses like a house of cards when you begin to reflect on it.

If no one gets hurt, then it is moral.

Imagine sitting down in a plaza a few feet away from the world's richest man. You hear him telling a friend that interest alone earns him millions every day. He goes on to say that on one occasion he actually misplaced a million dollars in cash and never bothered to call the police because it wouldn't be worth the effort. He makes his point even more concrete by saying that if he lost that kind of cash in the future, it would be his own fault for carrying it around, and he would never report it missing.

You can't believe your ears. A million dollars is nothing to him!

The billionaire then gets up, walks away, and drives off in a limo, never to be seen again. As you are about to leave the plaza, you notice a briefcase under the bench where the rich man had been sitting. You pick it up and look inside. To your amazement, you find one million dollars.

What do you do?

Would you keep it because the rich man actually admitted he would never miss it and that he would never report it? No one is hurt by keeping it — you heard the rich man say that in his own words. You may even think that good could come from keeping it. You might give some to the poor and pay your own bills.

Or would you give it back? After all, it's not your money. Would you feel guilty spending it? Is taking something that isn't yours wrong only if someone gets hurt by it, or is it fundamentally wrong?

Many, many people would not give the money back. But put this decision to the test for a moment.

- Would he want other people making decisions about his losses without his consent?

- Can you be sure that he would not change his mind?

- What if that particular money was earmarked for a charity and the rich man decided to forgo the gift when he realized he'd lost the money?

There is always a price that someone pays for immorality, even when it appears that no one is hurt. Once you start down the path of moral relativism, you eventually become comfortable justifying all your behaviors, and that makes winning the world impossible.

It is impossible to speculate exactly how people do or don't get hurt by the immoral acts of any individual, but there is always someone who does get hurt. Pornography is a prime example of this. Advocates of pornography claim that it hurts no one because looking at images is something that people can do in the privacy of their own homes. But that is not what the record shows. In extreme examples, men who become porn addicts are more likely to get divorced, have affairs, and commit sexual crimes than men who stay clear of porn. Other effects include loss of interest in their wives, or manipulating them against their will to emulate behaviors seen in pornography.

Relativism affects the economy as well. There are thousands of attempts to collect illegitimate insurance money every year. People who make these claims often do so because they consider the source of the payout to be a faceless, over-rich company, not an individual like them. They ignore that the result is higher premiums to make up for illegitimate payouts. Honest people pay millions of dollars to insurance companies to staff fraud protection departments, and if the department fails to catch fraud, then honest people pay for illegitimate claims. In some cases, in fact, even *legitimate claims* are not honored because, with so much fraud going on, the insurance companies become excessively vigilant and falsely accuse people of making phony claims. (Of course, the pendulum of relativism swings both ways. The desire to make an extra buck has inspired many an insurance company to fail to live up to their end of the bargain as well.)

Immorality always hurts somebody, even if that somebody is simply the perpetrator. Making immoral choices warps your conscience and leads you down a dark path, resulting in emptiness. It will eventually strip you of the gratification that comes from living with purpose and meaning.

If everyone agrees to it, then it is moral.

Some people argue that if all parties consent to something then it is moral, but this philosophy holds water like a sieve. According to this philosophy, it would be moral for a thirty-five-year-old man to have sex with a consenting fifteen-year-old-girl just because they both agree to it. This is obviously false. The fact that two parties agree to a certain act does not change the nature of the act. Therefore, it is often the act itself that will determine the morality of the issue.

Some people argue that life is filled with exceptions and that special situations call for special exceptions, but the nature of an act supersedes exceptions. *Of course* there are complex moral issues, but when all of the veneer is removed, a basic moral truth can always be found at the core.

I had a conversation with a colleague who claimed that there is no such thing as an absolute moral truth. He said, for example, that it is moral for married couples to have relations with other people as long as both parties agree, but it would be immoral if they did not agree. But, I asked, what if they both agree and then one of them changes his or her mind? Is it then moral or immoral? Even for a relativist, the water gets way too muddy on these types of issues. But my colleague stuck to his guns and claimed that changing one's mind would be morally acceptable and that "judging" the person from a moral perspective for changing his mind about becoming more liberal in the relationship would be wrong. When I asked him if it would be permissible for his girlfriend to change her mind and begin to sleep around, somehow he found religion and claimed that to be unacceptable! Another problem with morality-by-agreement is that it isn't always clear who should have the right to set the rules. Would it be moral for a student to copy answers from a nearby student during a test if the other student agrees? Would it be moral if a teacher and student agreed to let the student cheat? These may seem like ridiculous questions, but relativism is ridiculous to begin with, and most issues involving relativism boil down to equally ridiculous claims, once you cut away the superficial details.

It is not always easy to find the moral conclusion to situations. It takes considered thought in some circumstances. Take time out to form your understanding of the natural law by studying sound philosophy, testing theories, and remaining open to the truth when you find it. Soon you will begin to see patterns in the natural law that will increase your clarity and put you well on your way to winning the world.

❧ Conclusion ❧

MOVING FORWARD

THE OLD SAYING goes that "God can write straight with crooked lines." As far as winning the world is concerned, it doesn't matter what your past looks like. None of us is perfect, and all of us have lost our way a few times. But both your negative and positive experiences have become a part of who you are. Even the regrets you have in life can be used for good. Just think of it this way: any negatives you've had will make your comeback story even better.

Frank Abagnale Jr. is a great example of this. His story was popularized by the movie *Catch Me If You Can*. In just a few short years, Frank cashed over $2,500,000 in fake checks (that's in 1960s dollars!) in over twenty-six countries. Among other scams, he impersonated an emergency room physician, Pan Am pilot, Harvard grad, and attorney. For five years, he ran from the law. When he was caught, he was found guilty and sentenced to jail. And he managed to accomplish all of this before the age of twenty-two. He was using his intelligence and his gifts, but he was losing his soul in the process.

In a twist of fate, Frank's prison sentence was reduced when he was asked to assist the FBI in identifying forgeries and other fraudulent bank practices. He parlayed that opportunity by starting his own very successful fraud prevention consulting company. In fact, his services are what most banks and consumers rely on today to ensure that our checks are handled safely. Frank had a past, and he couldn't hide it. He now uses the lessons he learned from his experience committing crimes to prevent them. Is your past really any worse than Frank's? You can wring your hands over the past, or you can get busy making things right by taking action right now.

Studies show that infants who are held, nurtured, and loved grow faster and are healthier than babies who get proper nourishment but no attention. It's in the nature of a baby to need love, so babies are at their best in a loving environment. In a similar way, you have basic mental, emotional, and spiritual needs that can be met only by nourishing yourself with personal challenges.

Although I don't know you personally, I am excited for your future. You have so much ahead of you. I know this because I have helped countless people from all walks of life make a better plan for themselves. If you take your obligation to win the world seriously, then you *will* get results. As the preceding chapters explain, you must seek out existential gratification, get on a course to become an expert, dig down deep into your resolve, and go beyond your capacity in order to reach your potential.

You will get results in all areas of your life if you practice these concepts. With growth and success, you will face new challenges, but you'll be able to manage them as long as you remain humble. Remember again that humility is best defined as *precision truth about oneself.* Humility is not wimpiness or self-defeatism. Humility is the greatest virtue anyone could ever possess. Research in several fields has empirically proved this. No doubt, humility has always been promoted by religious figures, but in recent years, psychology, education, and business experts have all discovered, through research, that the strongest and most resilient people are humble. Humility will keep you ready for whatever challenges come your way.

One great way to reduce pride in your life and to increase humility is to focus on the needs of others, in large and subtle ways. The late Victor Frankl observed, during his time in Auschwitz, that the prisoners who gave what little bread or comfort they had to others remained healthier and survived even if they were experiencing hunger or pain themselves. Focusing on something larger than themselves helped keep them grounded and determined to survive.

Daily reflections on humility and gratitude are essential. Take time out every day to ask yourself the following questions:

1. Did you perform up to your capacity today? Would others say the same? Did you hold back because you were self-conscious or overconfident? How can you correct that tomorrow?

2. Were your thoughts about your own needs so dominant that you failed to step outside of yourself to help others?

3. Were you grateful today for the little things (as well as the big things) you have, or did you reflect only on what you don't have?

4. Are you committed to changing these things even if you have failed in the past?

Winning anything worthwhile is a challenge. Great victories are usually a result of winning several small battles. It is a lifelong commitment. No matter where you are in life right now, there is still time to find victory. It is in your nature to win the world. Whether you know it or not, you were made with incredible precision for an incredible purpose. It is now up to you to explore the "features and benefits" of your personality, temperament, interests, and inclinations.

Keep a clean conscience so that you see the truth. One of the greatest ways to get a better image of yourself is to put yourself in the "audience" of your life. When people see themselves recorded on video, they often comment about their appearance and their voice. "I don't really look and sound like that ... do I?" But the video reveals the truth.

Similarly, you should step outside and see yourself as a student while you are simultaneously the instructor. What advice do you have for yourself? Are you a malleable subject ready to change in order to grow? Or are you rigid and unwilling to take your own advice? Seek out people who are your seniors who are well on their way to winning the world. Follow them. Learn from them and gain wisdom vicariously through their experiences. Then return the favor by leading others.

When you put this book down, you'll be faced with a decision. You will decide to take action on your pursuit to win the world, or you will not. It is really that simple.

For most of you, the decision will be made within seconds of closing the book. Great decisions are often made in a split second.

In a split second, my friend Andy Meier made a decision to be great, and he will never regret the outcome even though he lives with it every day. Eight months prior to my writing this page, he was a passenger on a tour bus in Bosnia with his family. In a matter of seconds, an exciting trip turned into an unimaginable horror. He looked up and saw a semi truck coming straight at the tour bus. In an instant, he realized that his four-year-old son was standing unprotected from the danger. He compromised his own safety to protect his son as the truck slammed into their bus and sent it down a ravine and into a riverbed.

Andy's son walked away injury-free, but Andy still sits in a wheelchair as I write these words. It is difficult to describe the pain that his family feels, but I know one thing. His decision to save his son is one he will never regret, no matter how difficult things get. As he and his heroic wife, Elizabeth, suffer through this difficult time, they can do so with a clean conscience. Andy was a great man before the accident, but he never could have become as great as he is today without making that decision to win the world by saving his son.

I believe that Andy will walk again, but regardless of when that happens, his example is already a complete lesson: The decision to do the right thing can always be made swiftly no matter the consequence, because doing the right thing should always be your default response to all of life's challenges.

You may not be called upon today to do something heroic and life-threatening, but you are being given the chance to seize the opportunities you have to win the world for yourself and those you love. Make the decision to win the world right now. Even if the path sounds difficult, it is incredibly rewarding and it is the only one that will bring you the joy that you desire.

About the Author

Dave Durand (*www.davedurand.com*) has been named by *Leadership Excellence* magazine as one of the nation's top one hundred minds on the personal side of leadership. He is on the radio weekly in forty markets nationwide giving advice on business and personal growth issues. Dave is also the author of the national bestseller *Perpetual Motivation,* which was an Amazon #1 bestseller in its field for three months.

Dave was the youngest person in Cutco's fifty-five-year history to be inducted into the company's Hall of Fame. He eventually oversaw the Canadian operation and a fifteen-state region in the United States. For the past sixteen years Dave has researched, observed, and coached in excess of a hundred thousand individuals from all walks of life — sales representatives, Fortune 500 CEOs, secretaries, educators, small business owners, and even stay-at-home parents. Drawing from the lessons of his research, he has given over twelve hundred presentations in various industries on motivation, time management, ethical business, leadership, and other major topics.

Dave lives with his wife and children in Pewaukee, Wisconsin.

Join TEAM DURAND COACHING today

Dave Durand will coach you on Winning the World
without Losing Your Soul

*Receive two lessons on CD each month
and master your leadership skills:*

- Balance in life and work
- Decision making and judgment
- Living in virtue and overcoming vice
- Communication skills
- Planning and execution
- And much more . . .

Visit *www.davedurand.com* for more details.
Click on Team Durand Coaching

Of Related Interest

Dave Durand
PERPETUAL MOTIVATION
*How to Light Your Fire and Keep It Burning
in Your Career and in Life*

- ◆ Achieve more with less effort!
- ◆ Become a "legacy achiever" who makes a difference.
- ◆ Empower your life and excel in your career, finances,
  family and relationships, health, and more!

Dave Durand walks you step by step through the "formula
for motivation." He goes beyond the feel-good solutions
and gets to the heart of what really motivates you and
keeps you motivated, perpetually! Using sharp and fresh
anecdotes and drawing from his study of legacy achiev-
ers, Durand shows us that highly motivated people use a
strategy for success that doesn't involve any more effort
than you already invest. He demonstrates that motivation
is more about strategy and focus than about effort. Read
this book today to unlock your motivational power.

"*Perpetual Motivation* cuts to the core of what really mo
tivated top performers."
                          --Dan Jansen, Olympic Gold Medalist

"*Perpetual Motivation* goes far deeper than the flood of
other books on that topic. A must read!"
                   — Eric Laine, Chairman/CEO Alcas Corporation

0-8245-2386-5, cloth

crossroad

Of Related Interest

Margaret Benefiel
THE SOUL OF A LEADER
How to Lead Resiliently and Effectively

While twenty-first-century leaders are rewarded for their drive, decisiveness, productivity, and long work hours, Margaret Benefiel shows that too often the soul goes unnourished, resulting in harm to the leader and to the organization the leader serves. Like gardeners trying to improve the health of a tree while ignoring the roots, leadership scholars, by and large, have been blind to a significant dimension of leadership.

Building upon the tremendous success of her first book, *The Soul at Work, The Soul of a Leader* pays attention to the roots, helping leaders keep their souls as alert as their minds and bodies. Benefiel's decade and a half of study, practice, and worldwide lecturing have culminated in the practical principles of soulful leadership that she offers here.

Interviews with Tom and Kate Chappell (of Tom's of Maine), Bob Glassman (Wainwright Bank, Boston), Desmond Tutu, and The Edge (of the rock band U2), supported with guided questions in each section, make this book an essential addition to the bookshelf of anyone interested in finding the right path, avoiding detours, and persevering to the end.

0-8245-2480-2, paperback

crossroad

Of Related Interest

Frank J. Hanna
WHAT YOUR MONEY MEANS
(*And How to Use it Well*)

"This thought-provoking book should not be missed. Frank Hanna shows you how to appreciate the hidden value of wealth." — Raymond Arroyo, *New York Times* bestselling author

"Am I spending my money as I should?" "Am I living my life as I should?" We all ask ourselves these questions, but the pressures of business and daily life seem to keep us from finding sure answers.

"Frank Hanna digs through centuries of wise thought from Socrates, Plato, and Tacitus to Henry Ford and P. J. O'Rourke to crystallize an intelligent approach to allocating and enjoying wealth. The journey through this book edifies those with lots of wealth — or little. No one should give away a cent without reading this book first." — Foster Friess, founder of Brandywine Funds

0-8245-2520-2, cloth

Check your local bookstore for availability.
To order directly from the publisher,
please call 1-800-707-0670 for Customer Service
or visit our Web site at *www.cpcbooks.com*.
For catalog orders, please send your request to the address below.

THE CROSSROAD PUBLISHING COMPANY
16 Penn Plaza, Suite 1550
New York, NY 10001

crossroad